ONE HUNDRED HILL WALKS AROUND EDINBURGH

ONE HUNDRED HILL WALKS AROUND EDINBURGH

JOHN CHALMERS

and

DEREK STOREY

MAINSTREAM PUBLISHING

First published in Great Britain in 1990 by
MAINSTREAM PUBLISHING COMPANY
(EDINBURGH) LTD
7 Albany Street
Edinburgh EH1 3UG

Reprinted 1991

ISBN 1 85158 330 0 (paper)

British Library Cataloguing in Publication Data:

Chalmers, John,   Storey, Derek
  One Hundred hillwalks around Edinburgh.
  1. Edinburgh region. – Visitors' guides
  I. Title II. Storey, Derek
  914.134

ISBN 1-85158-330-0

Typeset in 10pt Times by Bookworm Typesetting Ltd, Edinburgh
Printed in Great Britain by Martin's of Berwick-Upon-Tweed

CONTENTS

	Page
Map of areas covered	6
About this book	8
Notes	10
Abbreviations	12
Gaelic and Scots words	13
Symbols on sketch maps	14

The Walks

Edinburgh and West Lothian	17
Pentland Hills	29
Lammermuir Hills	53
Moorfoot Hills	79
Minchmoor and Eildon Hills	105
Manor Hills	115
Ettrick Hills	133
Cloich Hills and Broughton Heights	147
Moffat Hills	157
Central Southern Uplands	167
Ochil Hills	197
Lomond Hills and Cleish Hills	223
Central and Tayside Regions	233

Author's comments and hints

Getting to the start	243
Action and attitude	244
Clothing	245
Kit	246
Companions	248
Weather	249
Safety	250
Rights and responsibilities	251
Index of places	253

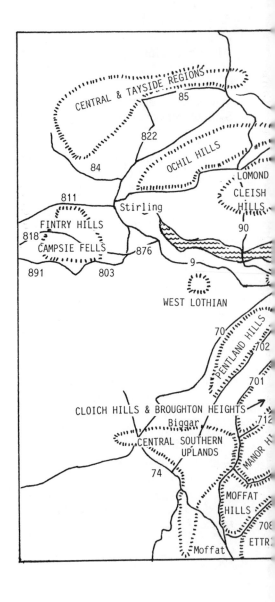

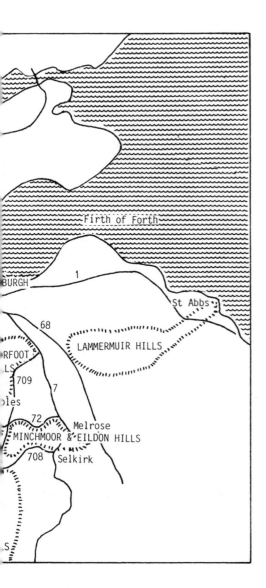

Firth of Forth

BURGH

1

St Abbs

68

LAMMERMUIR HILLS

RFOOT
LS

709

7

les

72

Melrose

MINCHMOOR & EILDON HILLS

708

Selkirk

S

ABOUT THIS BOOK

The interest in hill walking is growing steadily as the benefits and enjoyments of the open air with pleasant exercise become more appreciated. For regular participation it is necessary to have hill walks which can be made in a single day, using a car to get to the starting point. This book is written to meet this need for walkers living in Edinburgh and the south-east of Scotland. It is a companion volume to the book *One Hundred Hill Walks Around Glasgow*. Although the areas covered by these books overlap, with few exceptions the walks described in this book differ from those of the Glasgow book.

It is a practical guide to be used in planning walks and when on the hills. It enables the reader to choose between far and near from home, and between short and long distances on foot. It also allows a choice between high climbs and not-so-high climbs. It tells how to shorten each walk should this become necessary. Remember that hill walking is for all ages.

One of the appeals of hill walking is the solitude – the getting away from the bustle of town life. Many of the walks described ensure this by giving routes which are not often walked, which have no paths or signposts, but are attractive just because of that. Hill walkers will quickly devise variations of their own making, to develop their urge for exploration, their need for isolation, and their desire for achievement.

Most Edinburgh people have heard of the Pentland Hills, the Lammermuir Hills, and the Moorfoot Hills, but there are also the Ochils and Lomond Hills to the north, the Clydesdale and Lowther Hills to the south-west, the Campsies and the Fintry Hills to the west, and the Manor Hills and those around Broughton and Moffat to the south. And there are many more, including a few in the city itself. All these areas are covered in this book which the authors hope will satisfy its readers.

So go ahead and enjoy your walks in the hills.

NOTES

1.   The sketch maps are to give a quick visual idea of each walk. They are not to scale. They do not replace the Ordnance Survey maps, the appropriate sheet of which should always be carried. It is recommended that the 1:50,000 Landranger Series be used. The relevant map for each walk is stated at the beginning of each description. Note that, very occasionally, a route will require two maps.

2.   The "Distance from city centre" is as it says, but remember it is also the same distance back, so have petrol in the tank for double the distance stated.

3.   The "Walking distance" includes an allowance for the continuous variations from the route as it would be measured on the map. It is always necessary on a hill walk to make short detours to avoid bog, rocks, hillocks, etc. While an allowance has been made for this, the resultant figure must be approximate.

4.   The "Amount of climbing" is the sum of all the uphill sections of the route.

5.   Distances given within texts are approximations meant for guidance only.

6.   Compass directions and bearings given in the text are based on Ordnance Survey "Grid North". The prevailing magnetic variation, given at the top of Ordnance Survey maps, should be taken into account. To do this, add the magnetic variation to the given bearing, or point the magnetic needle to magnetic north (i.e. north on the dial less the magnetic variation).

7.   Conditions in the countryside change; new forests are planted, fences are erected, new roads are laid over

agricultural land, etc., so you may find variations from what is written in the text, but these should not prevent you from finding a way round them. While every endeavour has been made to be accurate in all details, should some errors have crept in we apologise for these in advance. No responsibility can be accepted for any loss, etc. caused by an inaccuracy; and the fact that a walk is described in this book does not infer a right of way nor does it guarantee that access will always be available.

8.   A few of the walks are not strictly on hills, but they are of the type which hillwalkers can enjoy, perhaps on "rest" days or because of inclement weather.

9.   Readers are warned that low flying jets are common in most areas covered by this book. The sudden, intense noise can give walkers quite a start, especially when they fly at or below the walker's level.

10.   Everyone walks at their own pace. However, a reasonable estimate of walking time for an adult may be made by allowing 12 minutes for each kilometre plus an additional minute for each ten metres of altitude to be climbed. Also allow a ten-minute rest stop for each hour of walking.

ABBREVIATIONS

km	kilometres
ml	miles
m	metres
ft	feet
yd	yards
NN-, NO-, NS-, NT-	National Grid reference
N, S, E, W	Directions of the compass
(-m/-ft)	Height above sea level
TP	Triangulation pillar
Munro	Any mountain in Scotland 3000 feet or more in height. Named after Sir Hugh T. Munro, Bart
Corbett	Any mountain in Scotland 2500 feet to 2999 feet in height. Named after Mr J. Rooke Corbett

GAELIC AND SCOTS WORDS

Word	Pronounced	Meaning
a', an	an, ahn	the, this (often used before names of places)
allt	alt	a burn, a river
beag	bake	little, small
bealach	by alach	a pass, or lowest point, between hills
beinn	bane	a mountain
bin	bin	a hill (a form of "ben")
carn	karn	a cairn, a rocky hill
col	cawl	a gap between two mountains, a bealach
corrie	cawri	a hollow in a hillside
creag	kragg	a crag, a rock
cruach	croo-ach	a stack
cruachan	croo-a-han	a conical hill
dod	dawd	a bare hill with a rounded top
dubh, dhubh	doo (short)	black, dark
dun	doon (long)	a hillock, a fort
fell	fel	a rocky hill
knowe	now	a knoll
lane	lain	a waterway between two lochs
law	law	a rounded hill, usually isolated
maol	may ol	a bare top
meall	myall	a rounded hill
meikle	meekle	large
mor, mhor	mo-ar	great, big
muir	moor	an alternative spelling of "moor"
rig	rig	a ridge
sgorr, squrr	skawr, skoor	a rocky, pointed hill
spout	spowt	a waterfall, especially coming from a cleft in rocks or a spring
sron	srawn	a peak, a spur
stell	stell	a circular, dry-stane sheep enclosure
stuc	stoog	a steep, rocky peak
tumulus	toomyoolus	a heap of earth covering prehistoric tomb (also called a "barrow" and "chambered cairn")

SYMBOLS ON SKETCH MAPS

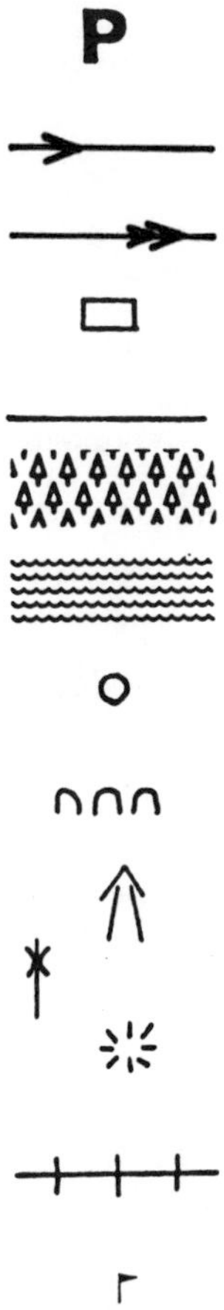

P   Parking place and start of walk

⟶   Route of walk

⟶⟶   Uphill

▭   Building

───   Fence or wall

Woodland

Water

◯   Hilltop

∩∩∩   Rocky face of hill

⩚   Overhead electric power line

⅄   Television or radar mast

☀   Archaeological site

─┼─┼─┼─   Railway

⌐   Golf course

THE WALKS

As indicated on page 11 the Walks described are not necessarily Right-of-Ways, but established routes are followed wherever possible. The attention of readers is also drawn to the section on page 251 regarding rights and responsibilities, and it is hoped that users of this book will take every care to avoid doing damage while following the routes, and so maintain and improve the good relationship that exists between walker and landowner in Scotland. In particular, it has been requested that walkers avoid the following hills during the lambing and/or bird nesting seasons:

Walk 10   King's Seat, Byrehope Mount and Craigengar;
Walk 11   Faw Mount and Mount Maw;
Walk 12   Black Hill.

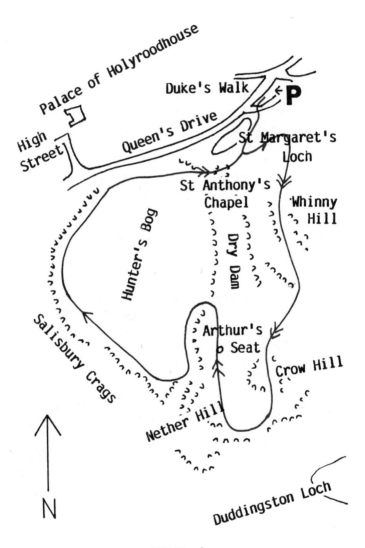

Palace of Holyroodhouse

Duke's Walk

P

High Street

Queen's Drive

St Margaret's Loch

St Anthony's Chapel

Whinny Hill

Hunter's Bog

Dry Dam

Arthur's Seat

Salisbury Crags

Crow Hill

Nether Hill

N

Duddingston Loch

WALK 1

EDINBURGH AND
WEST LOTHIAN

1. *Holyrood Park and Arthur's Seat*
Ordnance Survey map No: 66
Distance from city centre: 2km/1.3ml
Walking distance: 7.2km/4.5ml
Amount of climbing: 390m/1279ft

Few major cities can boast such a delightful area within the heart of the city. A must for all residents and visitors.

Use carpark off Duke's Walk, between St Margaret's Loch and Meadowbank entrance to park. NT278741. To get there go along High Street to Palace of Holyroodhouse then right, enter Park and go left along Queen's Drive to carpark just beyond St Margaret's Loch.

Take footpath beside the loch heading uphill towards St Anthony's Chapel (ruins). Just before the steep incline to the ruins turn back on to thin track that traverses above loch and carpark. Just beyond carpark, turn right on to wide grassy track between gorse bushes and climb up and over Whinny Hill.

On the far side of Whinny Hill is a valley up which the tourist route passes from Dunsapie Loch on the left to the summit of Arthur's Seat ahead and to the right. Directly ahead is Crow Hill. Descend into the valley then climb to the large pyramidal cairn on the summit of Crow Hill. From here there are stupendous views to the E of Edinburgh.

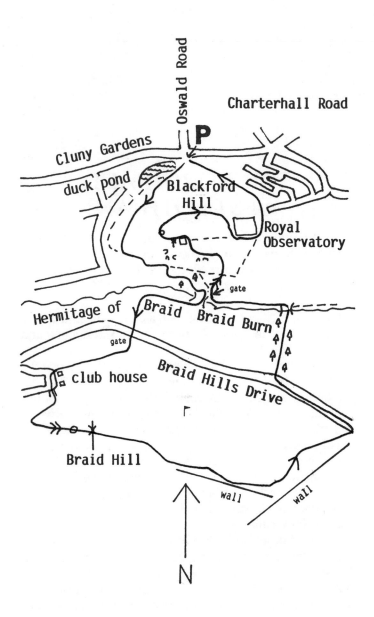

WALK 2

Descend steeply down the far side of Crow Hill to the top of the crags immediately above Duddingston Loch (a bird sanctuary). Take the narrow path along the top of the crags heading W. Just before the path begins to descend steeply, turn right up a gully to reach the top of Nether Hill. Continue directly ahead to the summit of Arthur's Seat (251m/823ft. TP. Viewfinder).

Take the main path (NE) off the summit then go left (NW) for about 50yd to a fork in the path. Here go left (W) to descend steeply down the side of the wide valley (Hunter's Bog) between Arthur's Seat and Salisbury Crags. Follow the path as it traverses S beneath the steep sides of Arthur's Seat to the saddle at the end of Salisbury Crags. Turn right here and follow the top of the crags for 1.5km/0.9ml. Just beyond Holyrood Palace, climb up to the ruins of St Anthony's Chapel then descent past St Margaret's Loch to the carpark.

To shorten the walk, follow the base of Arthur's seat N through Dry Dam, a small valley, back to St Margaret's Loch. Save 2.3km/1.4ml.

2. Blackford and Braid Hills

Ordnance Survey map No: 66
Distance from city centre: 4.9km/3ml
Walking distance: 9.6km/6ml
Amount of climbing: 262m/859ft

A short easy hill walk close to the centre of Edinburgh. Terrain mostly rough grass and gorse. Good paths throughout.

Park at entrance to Blackford Park at end of Cluny Gardens. NT255710. To get there, drive S along Lothian Road to Morningside then left at major junction beyond shops into Cluny Gardens.

Enter the Park, turn right and climb the steps adjacent to the duck pond to footpath. Follow path around Blackford Hill, above some allotments, then join a track beside a stone wall round to the S side of the hill. Pass

19

Arthur's Seat : walk 1

Salisbury Crags, Holyrood Park : walk 1

through a gap in the wall immediately beneath some crags on to a path through woodland down into Hermitage of Braid.

Cross the large wooden bridge over Braid Burn and follow path between iron railings to Braid Hills Drive. Pass through black metal gate opposite and climb directly ahead through gorse to golf course. Go right along edge of the golf course to the Club House. Walk along the road, pass the Club House, then climb one of the paths between the gorse bushes to summit of Braid Hill (280m/682ft. TP).

Head E, passing to left of radio mast, then around edge of golf course on a footpath then a bridle path beside a stone wall to Braid Hills Drive. Go left along the road for 500yd then right on a footpath through a line of trees into Hermitage of Braid. Cross bridge over burn then walk upstream to the next bridge (the one used earlier in the walk). Here go right, pass through a black swing gate then, after a few paces, turn off to the right again up a gully through some trees. At the top of the gully turn left and head up past the radio mast to the summit of Blackford Hill (164m/538ft. TP. Viewfinder).

Follow the ridge to the Royal Observatory. Walk along the road for a few yards then go left on footpath along the edge of the Park back down to the entrance.

To shorten the walk: (1) Omit Braid Hills. Turn around in Hermitage of Braid and climb to top of Blackford Hill. Save 7.2km/4.4ml. (2) Omit Blackford Hill by starting and finishing at Braid Hills Drive. Save 5.2km/3.2ml.

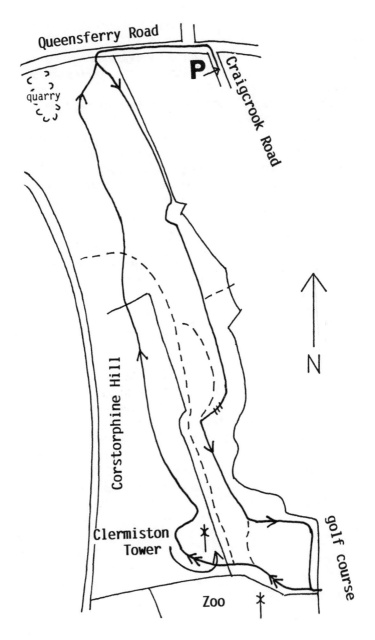

Queensferry Road

quarry

P

Craigcrook Road

Corstorphine Hill

Clermiston Tower

Zoo

golf course

N

WALK 3

3.   *Corstorphine Hill*

Ordnance Survey map No: 66

Distance from city centre: 5.5km/3.4ml

Walking distance: 7.3km/4.5ml

Amount of climbing: 124m/406ft

A short, pleasant stroll through mixed deciduous woodland.

Park car in Craigcrook Road, off Queensferry Road, near Davidson's Mains. NT207750. To get there, drive W from the city centre along the Queensferry Road (A90).

Walk W along Queensferry Road a few yards to a footpath signpost for "Corstorphine Hill and Clermiston Tower". Turn left and take the gravel track behind some houses along the edge of Corstorphine Hill. Continue along the path, past a footpath going off to the left and some open ground, then up some wooden steps. At the top turn left on to another path and follow this through the woods to a junction of footpaths. Here go left on a path overlooking a golf course until it stops abruptly at the golf course perimeter fence.

Climb a narrow path to the right, beside the fence and past a large boulder, to the metal railings of Edinburgh Zoo on the top of a ridge. A few paces to the left is a splendid view over the Forth. To continue go right beside the railings. At a fork keep left to pass close by a radio mast then descend some wooden steps to a multiple junction of paths.

Look up and to the right for another, higher, radio mast and take one of the paths heading up towards it. Close to the mast you will find Clermiston Tower. Walk past it and take one of the many paths along the ridge heading N and gradually descend until you eventually emerge on to the original path close to the Queensferry Road entrance.

To shorten the walk, on the outward path cut up to the right to one of the paths along the top of the ridge running back to the entrance.

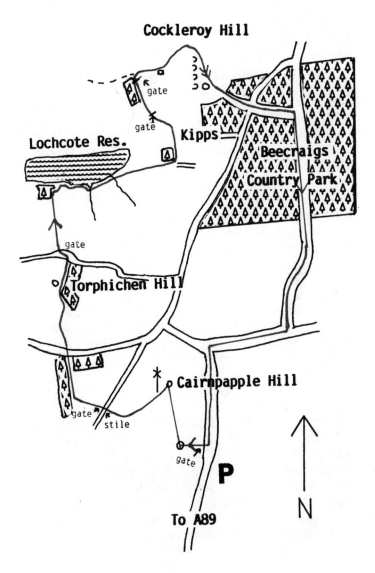

Cockleroy Hill

gate

gate

Lochcote Res.

Kipps

Beecraigs
Country Park

gate

Torphichen Hill

gate
stile

Cairnpapple Hill

gate

P

To A89

N

WALK 4

4. *Cairnpapple and Cockleroy Hills*

Ordnance Survey map No: 65

Distance from city centre: 29.3km/18.2ml

Walking distance: 17.4km/10.6ml

Amount of climbing: 230m/754ft

A pleasant, low level hill walk over grazing land and rough grassland with views stretching from Arran to the Bass Rock. There is a restored Bronze Age burial chamber (admission charge) on Cairnpapple Hill.

Leave car in small carpark next to viewfinder at Knock. NS990711. To get there, drive out to the Newbridge roundabout and take the A89. Turn right just beyond Bangour Hospital then second right. The carpark is on the right at the top of the hill.

After exploring the small hill with the viewfinder head N along the road for a few paces to a gate on the left. Pass through and climb up to the TP (312m/1023ft). Now head N across to Cairnpapple Hill (burial chamber, radio mast). Descend to the W along the radio mast access road to a gate and stile on`to an asphalt road.

Cross the road, go through the gate opposite, walk down to the woodland then bear right, following the trees, down to another road. Cross over and climb the wall opposite then head N (350°) beside a fence then stone wall across a shallow valley then up on to Torphichen Hill (220m/721ft).

Continue N to a minor road. Go through the gate opposite a yellow cottage and follow the track to small copse of trees overlooking Lothcote Reservoir. Turn right and follow an iron fence over a burn and fence to the next burn, then climb on to a cluster of small, gorse-covered hills. Scramble down N side, step over fence and cross field to gate. Go through gate and take farm road heading NNW (337°) to next gate. Pass through, turn right, pass a small ruin and head round to the N of Cockleroy Hill where it is possible to climb up to the summit (278m/911ft. TP. Viewfinder, fort).

Walk down the tourist track into the forest and follow

the arrows to an asphalt road. Cross over into Beecraigs Country Park and continue E through the forest to toilets, carpark and road. Follow the road S for 1.8km/1ml to a T-junction. Go right and take the next road to the left (signposted "Cairnpapple") back to the starting point.

To shorten the walk, (using a map) find a way back to the starting point from any of the roads that are crossed en route. Or, from the hills overlooking the Lothcote Reservoir, walk past the Kipps (ruin of tower plus adjacent farm) to the road then back to the car. Save 4.3km/2.7ml.

Caerketton Hill with ski-slopes : walk 5

Footpath near The Howe, Pentland Hills : walks 6 and 7

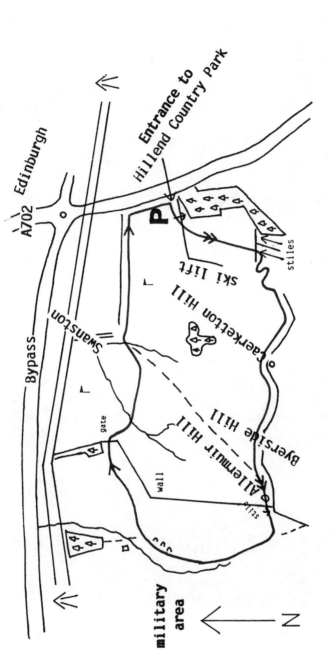

WALK 5

PENTLAND HILLS

5. *Caerketton and Allermuir Hills*
Ordnance Survey map No: 66
Distance from city centre: 8km/5ml
Walking distance: 11.7km/7.2ml
Amount of climbing: 450m/1476ft

Proximity to Edinburgh and the superb views make this a very popular walk.

Park car in lay-by just inside Hillend Country Park. NT250670. To get there, go by A702 (Biggar Road) to just past bypass (A720).

Walk up grassy bank on left then, at end of line of trees, bear left and climb steeply up the ridge parallel with the ski slope. At the top of ridge climb over right-hand stile and take zigzag path up to large cairn. From there follow fence and wall W, a little down-hill, then up to cairn on summit of Caerketton Hill (478m/1567ft).

Continue WSW (254°) on path beside fence, down into gully, then up over Byerside Hill and on to summit of Allermuir Hill (493m/1617ft. TP. View indicator).

Ahead is a military exercise area. If red flag is flying, or soldiers present, take shortcut described below. From Allermuir Hill climb over stile and head WNW (289°) beside a fence. Follow fence to left (192°) for about 100yd then bear right (252°), descend to saddle and

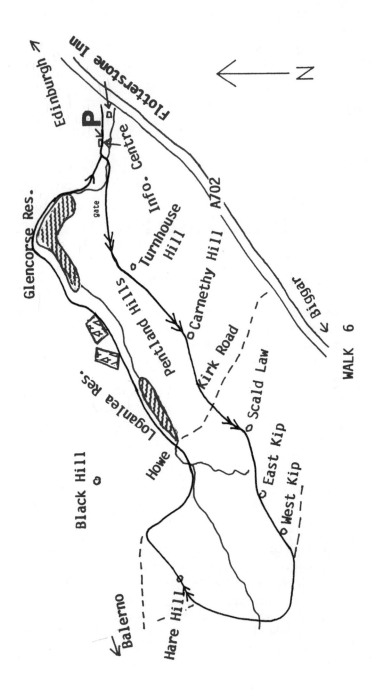

N

WALK 6

Edinburgh

Flotterstone Inn

A702

Biggar

Glencorse Res.

P

Info. Centre

gate

Turnhouse Hill

Pentland Hills

Carnethy Hill

Kirk Road

Scald Law

Loganlea Res.

East Kip

West Kip

Howe

Black Hill

Balerno

Hare Hill

join prominent track going N down the valley of Howden Burn. After 1.25km/0.8ml, beyond crags but before a small building, turn right on to path around hill, above some fenced areas of trees and head towards a spur of trees. Cross to a fence bordering a golf course. Climb over gate and go uphill beside fence for about 50yd then go left above golf course, over small burn, then alongside dismantled wall, then a line of white pegs, to join path coming down from Allermuir Hill beside Swanston Burn to Swanston.

Turn right in the village, to gate leading into Lothian-burn Golf Course. Follow right of way (signposted) beside the fence to Biggar Road (A702). Go S along this road for about 300yd to return to the entrance to Hillend Country Park.

Swanston is a tiny secluded hamlet of white-walled, thatched cottages, seemingly untouched by the passage of time. Robert Louis Stevenson spent much of his childhood here and used the village as the model for many of the locations described in his novels.

To shorten the walk, from the summit of Allermuir Hill take the footpath heading NE (42°) downhill to Swanston Burn and village, and so back to car. Save 3.2km/2ml.

6. Pentland Peaks
Ordnance Survey map No: 66
Distance from city centre: 12.5km/7.5ml
Walking distance: 25.8km/16ml
Amount of climbing: 770m/2525ft

Splendid walk with superb views along main ridge of the Pentland Hills.

Use carpark next to Flotterstone Countryside Information Centre. NT234631. To get there, go along A702 (Biggar Road) for 5km/3ml beyond bypass (A720) to Flotterstone. Drive past the inn to the Information Centre.

Turnhouse Hill from Flotterstone : walk 6

The "Kirk Road", Pentland Hills : walks 6 and 8

Walk along the road past the Countryside Information Centre. Where the road bears right, away from the stream, go straight ahead, through a gate and past a picnic site on the left. Then cross the bridge over a burn, turn right, walk over some ground churned up by cattle and, in a few paces, ford a tributary of the main stream and climb the ridge rising between the streams. Take the well-trodden path climbing steeply to the summit of Turnhouse Hill (506m/1660ft). Descend on a path heading SSW (204°) and climb the ridge ahead to the summit of Carnethy Hill (576m/1889ft). The enormous cairn on the summit is thought to have been used for sun worship in the distant past.

Descend towards WSW (250°) to saddle between Carnethy Hill and Scald Law. Across this saddle runs the "Kirk Road", a pass through the hills once used by Penicuik parishioners living on the far side of the Pentland Hills. Go through the gap in the fence and climb to the summit of Scald Law (579m/1899ft. TP), the highest point in the Pentland Hills.

Continue on path heading SW (235°). At a fork just below the summit go right, traversing around South Black Hill, then down to a saddle and up over the cone-shaped hills of East Kip and West Kip. Below West Kip join a prominent footpath heading WNW (282°) for about 800yd then N across a wide valley to the base of Hare Hill.

Leave the main footpath here and climb to the top of Hare Hill (449m/1472ft), then descend through heather heading ESE (118°) to a footpath. (If you reach a burn, you've gone too far!) Follow the path left, down into a deep gully between Hare Hill and Black Hill. At the bottom go right on a well-trodden path (Kirk Road) to The Howe, a farmhouse at the upper end of Loganlea Reservoir. Now take the access road past Loganlea and Glencourse Reservoir back to Flotterstone.

To shorten the walk, from the saddle between Carnethy Hill and Scald Law, turn right on to "Kirk Road" to rejoin the route at The Howe. Save 9.1km/5.6ml.

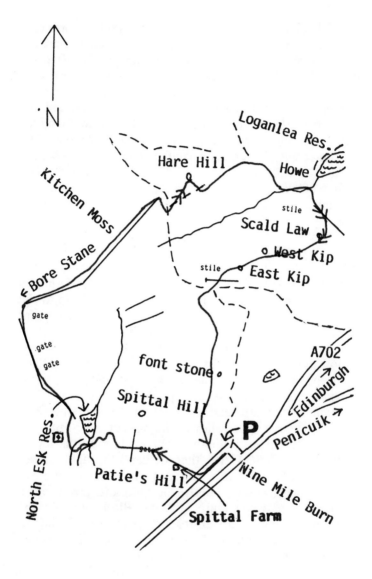

WALK 7

7. *Bore Stane and Scald Law*

Ordnance Survey map No: 65 or 72
Distance from city centre: 20km/12.5ml
Walking distance: 25km/15.4ml
Amount of climbing: 698m/2289ft

A long walk over desolate moors and some of the highest peaks in the Pentland Hills. Good paths but muddy in places.

Park car in Nine Mile Burn village. NT177577. To get there, go along A702 (Biggar Road) for 13km/8ml beyond bypass (A720).

Walk S through village to signpost for "Spittal Farm". Take farm road then follow the yellow arrows to the back of the farm. Go up track that ascends to the left of a small burn and on up to the saddle between Patie's Hill and Spittal Hill. Go through the gate in the wall and take the most prominent path (296°) to contour round Spittal Hill until the reservoir comes into view below. Descend steeply to the valley floor. Cross the dam wall and pass the keeper's house then walk along access road a short way to a left-hand bend. Turn right here on to footpath (signposted) across sheep grazing land to the right-hand corner of a clump of pine trees. Follow the path up valley, crossing to right of stream about 500yd beyond the trees, to prominent gate at the head of the valley. Bore Stane is a large rock on the far side of the gully to the left. The origin of its name is obscure.

Climb over the gate, turn right (66°), leaving the main path, and follow a wall for 3.2km/2ml over Kitchen Moss (moor) to the Balerno to Nine Mile Burn footpath (signposted) as it passes the foot of Hare Hill. Turn right on to the main path for 50 paces then turn left and climb Hare Hill (449m/1473ft). Cut down to the right (122°), across the heather, to a footpath. (If you reach a burn, you've gone too far!) Follow the path left down into a deep gully between Hare Hill and Black Hill. At the bottom go right on a path (Kirk Road) to The Howe. Cross the valley then climb over stile and ascend a very steep

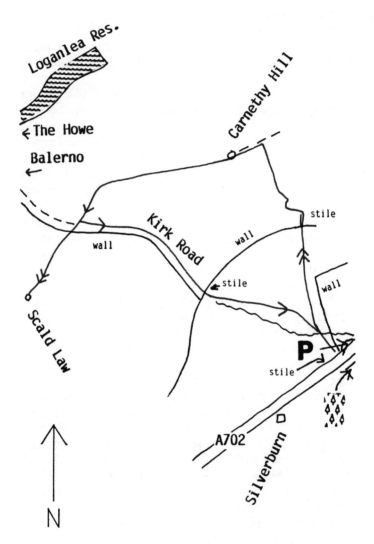

Loganlea Res.

← The Howe

Balerno ←

Carnethy Hill

stile

wall

Kirk Road

wall

← stile

wall

Scald Law

P

stile

A702

Silverburn

N

WALK 8

track up to the saddle between Scald Law and Carnethy Hill. Go through the gap in the fence on the right and climb steeply to the summit of Scald Law (579m/1899ft. TP), the highest point in the Pentland Hills.

Continue on path heading SW (235°). At a fork just below the summit go right to descend to a saddle then climb over the cone-shaped hills of East Kip and West Kip (550m/1806ft). Below West Kip cross a path and a stile over an electric fence. Here there are two paths to Nine Mile Burn, the lower one of which is signposted. Take the upper path by going right for a few paces then left up on to a ridge above a small plantation of trees. Follow the ridge down for 3km/1.8ml to Nine Mile Burn. Half way down you will pass the font stone, a large stone with a depression in it thought once to have supported a cross.

To shorten the walk, follow the signposted footpath from the base of Hare Hill back to Nine Mile Burn. Save 6.9km/4.2ml.

8. *Carnethy Hill and Scald Law*
Ordnance Survey map No: 66
Distance from city centre: 16km/10ml
Walking distance: 8.4km/5.2ml
Amount of climbing: 430m/1410ft

A relatively short hill walk on good paths over the two highest points in the Pentland Hills.

Park at lay-by on A702 shortly before Silverburn. NT211608. To get there, go by A702 (Biggar Road) to 8.4km/5.2ml past bypass (A720).

Directly above the parking place is Carnethy Hill; to the left is Scald Law with the "Kirk Road", an old pass through the mountains, running up the valley between them. Cross the stone wall by means of a stile a few yards from a footpath signpost pointing towards the hills. (This avoids a boggy area close to the signpost.) Head towards the hills, fording a stream and following the line of a wall. Do not take the path heading left between the two hills.

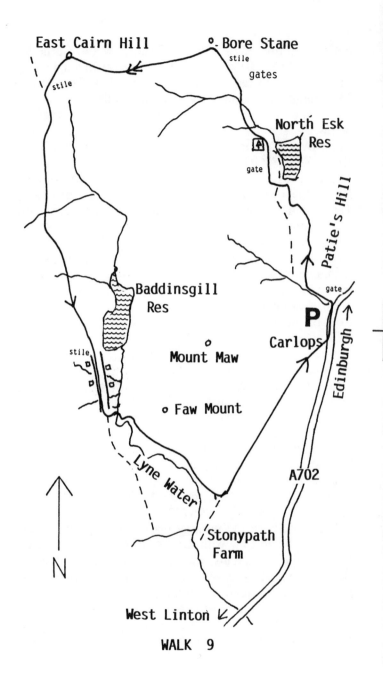

East Cairn Hill

Bore Stane

stile

gates

North Esk Res

gate

Patie's Hill

Baddinsgill Res

stile

Mount Maw

Faw Mount

gate

P

Carlops

Edinburgh

A702

Lyne Water

Stonypath Farm

N

West Linton

WALK 9

PENTLAND HILLS

At the end of the wall continue directly ahead on a steep grassy track between gorse bushes then head right (N 352°) across heather to another stile over a stone wall. Climb over this and go right beside the wall then turn left on to a steeply climbing zigzag path up on to the ridge. Here join a more prominent path from Turnhouse Hill and continue to the summit of Carnethy Hill (576m/1889ft).

On the summit of Carnethy Hill there is an enormous cairn which is thought to have been used for sun worship in the distant past. A few paces to the N of the cairn will provide a splendid view of Loganlea Reservoir far below.

Descend WSW (250°) from Carnethy Hill to the saddle between Carnethy Hill and Scald Law. Across this saddle runs the "Kirk Road", a pass through the hills once used by Penicuik parishioners living on the far side of the Pentlands. Go through the gap in the fence and climb steeply to the summit of Scald Law (579m/1899ft. TP).

Turn and descend from Scald Law down the same path that was used to go up. At the saddle turn right and follow the "Kirk Road" back down to the lay-by.

To shorten the walk, omit either Carnethy Hill or Scald Law. Save about 2.4km/1.5ml.

9. East Cairn Hill

Ordnance Survey map No: 65 or 72
Distance from city centre: 23.2km/14.3ml
Walking distance: 27km/16.6ml
Amount of climbing: 301m/987ft

A typical Pentland walk. Follows a popular trans-Pentland route, then climbs through heather, and later joins an old drove road.

Park car at Carlops Village Hall on edge of A702. NT161559. To get there, take the A702 SW towards Biggar as far as the village of Carlops.

Walk back along A702 to outskirts of Carlops and turn left on to footpath signposted "Kirknewton via Bore Stane". Follow the path through two swing gates close to cottage, then around Patie's Hill to North Esk Reservoir. Note: This well-trodden path is masked on OS map by Regional Boundary line.

Cross dam wall and pass reservoir keeper's house. At footpath signpost, about 100yd along access road, go through gate on right and cross sheep grazing land to right hand corner of a clump of pine trees then follow the footpath up the valley, crossing to the right of the stream 500yd beyond the trees. There are a few gates to climb on the way. At the head of the valley there is a gate and stile. Near the gully to the left is a large rock, the Bore Stane.

Turn left (SW 230°) and go uphill, beside a stone wall for most of the way, to the enormous cairn on the summit of East Cairn Hill (561m/1840ft). Continue past the cairn (215°) along a steeply descending path through heather to the saddle, Cauldstane Slap, between East Cairn Hill and West Cairn Hill. Climb over stile at footpath signposts and follow path then track towards West Linton.

At Baddinsgill Reservoir climb over stile on to an asphalt road and walk along this, past a few houses and over two streams, to footpath signpost for "Carlops via Stonypath". Move on to footpath and descend steeply to wooden bridge over Lyne Water. Cross over and follow the river bank downstream around sheep grazing enclosure then climb up over wooden walkway to join a bridlepath heading S (174°) around Faw Mount to Stonypath Farm. Go through farm and follow road round left to junction with three footpath signs. Take track towards Carlops passing through Pentlands Trekking Centre and emerging on to A702 on outskirts of Carlops.

To shorten the walk, return from Bore Stane by outward route. Save 12.3km/7.6ml.

South Black Hill (left) and Scald Law : walk 6

Whiteadder Reservoir : walks 15 and 22

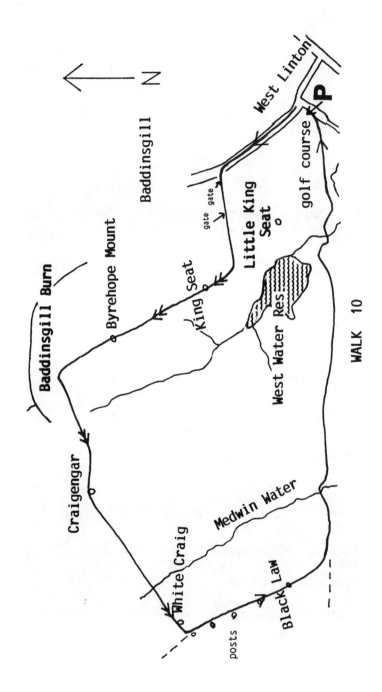

N

West Linton

Baddinsgill

Baddinsgill

Baddinsgill Burn

Byrehope Mount

Craigengar

gate gate

King Seat

Little King Seat

West Water Res

White Craig

Medwin Water

posts

Black Law

golf course

P

WALK 10

10. Byrehope Mount and Craigengar

Ordnance Survey map No: 65 or 72

Distance from city centre: 28km/17.3ml

Walking distance: 27.3km/17ml

Amount of climbing: 506m/1659ft

A long walk over several hills. Terrain mostly rough grassland or heather with very few paths.

Park car on edge of road close to West Linton Golf Course. If not busy, Golf Club may give permission to park in their carpark. NT141521. To get there, take the A702 (Biggar Road) as far as West Linton. Turn right at the signpost for Baddinsgill then, in 0.8km/0.5ml, left to the Golf Course.

Go along road towards Baddinsgill, over cattle grid and uphill, then through metal gate on left into sheep grazing land. Walk parallel with gully on the left, through another metal gate, then follow fence up and over King Seat (463m/1518ft). On the far side, leave fence and climb over rough grassland to summit of Byrehope Mount (534m/1753ft). From here follow another fence NW (325°) down long ridge to cairn and a 90° turn in the fence. Some rocks near here provide a useful shelter for a brew up.

Strike out through heather heading SW down to orange gas pipe-line (No 395) then climb up through heather to summit of Craigengar (518m/1699ft). There is a narrow path over to right, away from fence, but it is difficult to find. Descend from summit cairn down ridge (244°) towards White Craig, a steep round hill with a tall cairn on top visible for some considerable distance. Cross fence and stream (Medwin Water) at end of ridge then climb to summit of White Craig (434m/1423ft).

A solitary post on saddle between White Craig and Darlees Rig (226° from White Craig) marks the Crosswood to Dolphinton footpath. Descend to post then take path (very indistinct for the first kilometre – a few further posts, at about 200yd intervals mark line of path) SSE (156°) over to Black Law, past the Covenanter's Grave

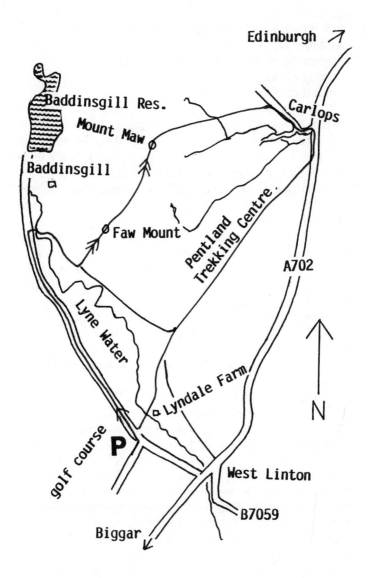

Edinburgh ↗

Carlops

Baddinsgill Res.

Mount Maw

Baddinsgill

Faw Mount

Pentland Trekking Centre.

A702

Lyne Water

N

Lyndale Farm

golf course

P

West Linton

B7059

Biggar

WALK 11

and down to gravel farm track. Walk E along this track for 5km/3ml to North Slipperfield Farm then along asphalt access road past West Linton Golf Course to Clubhouse.

To shorten the walk, from Byrehope Mount or Craigengar, descend into the valley between the two hills and follow the rough muddy track down to West Water Reservoir then on to North Slipperfield. Save 10.9km/7ml from the former, or 5.8km/3.6ml from the latter.

11. Mount Maw

Ordnance Survey map No: 65 or 72
Distance from city centre: 28km/17.3ml
Walking distance: 18km/11ml
Amount of climbing: 354m/1161ft

An interesting walk over rough sheep grazing land climbing to a height of 535m/1754ft. Returns along undulating farm tracks.

Park car on edge of road close to West Linton Golf Course. If not busy, Golf Club may give permission to park in their carpark. NT141521. To get there, take the A702 (Biggar Road) SW as far as West Linton. Turn right at the signpost for Baddinsgill then left to the golf course.

Walk along Baddinsgill road for 3km/1.8ml to the footpath signpost for "Carlops via Stonypath". Move on to the footpath and descend steeply to a wooden bridge over Lyne Water. Cross over and follow the river downstream around a sheep grazing enclosure then climb up over a wooden walkway and join a bridlepath heading S (174°). At the highest point, where a stone wall comes down the hill, turn left and follow the wall and fence up over Faw Mount then continue up to the TP on Mount Maw (535m/1754ft). Head down along a ridge (15°) to a small rise then turn E and descend to a gravel road thence on to the village of Carlops.

Go S along the A702 for about 200yd then take a track

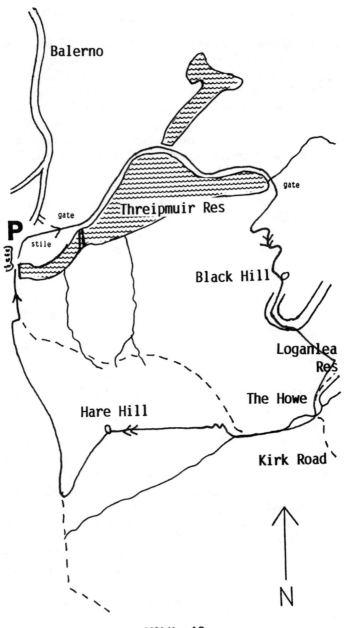

Balerno

Threipmuir Res

gate

P

gate

stile

stile

Black Hill

Loganlea Res

The Howe

Hare Hill

Kirk Road

N

WALK 12

on the right (212°), past some wooden cottages and through the Pentland Trekking Centre, to a junction with three footpath signposts. Follow the sign for West Linton but go right at a fork in the track and descend to Lyndale Farm. Pass through the farm, over Lyne Water, then SW along a short track to the Baddinsgill road. The starting point is about 200yd to the left.

It is not practicable to shorten this walk.

12. Black Hill

Ordnance Survey map No: 65 or 66
Distance from city centre: 15.6km/9.7ml
Walking distance: 16km/9.9ml
Amount of climbing: 428m/1403ft

A pleasant ramble around Threipmuir Reservoir (renowned for its bird life) and two overlooking hills. Heavy going up Black Hill, but easier elsewhere.

Park car within Red Moss Nature Reserve, 3.2km/2ml S of Balerno. NT165637. To get there, drive SW on the A70 to Balerno. Enter Balerno via Bridge Road and turn first left after Balerno High School into Main Street. Continue along this road as it becomes Mansfield Road then Cockburn Road. After 3km/2ml from the A70, pass the Marchbank Hotel then turn left into Red Moss Nature Reserve. Drive as far as authorised vehicles are allowed and park in the small carpark.

Climb over the stile on the edge of the road and take track heading E (74°) through woodland then through gate and across grazing land to Threipmuir Reservoir. Walk beside the water to dam wall, cross over and turn right to continue along the water's edge to a second dam. Cross over to reach a metal gate and pumphouse. Go about 30yd up a gully behind the pumphouse to two small concrete posts, turn right (210°) on to a narrow ascending path through heather for about 200yd, then turn left and zigzag up the steep slopes to small cairn on top of Black Hill (499m/1636ft).

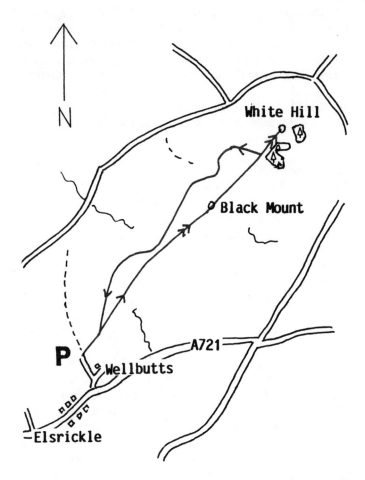

N

White Hill

Black Mount

A721

P

Wellbutts

Elsrickle

WALK 13

Leave the cairn on path heading SSW (206°). You will soon meet a gravel road (not marked on OS maps). Walk down this road for about 400yd to a left-hand bend. Leave the road here and continue directly ahead on a steeply descending, muddy track towards small dam wall on edge of Loganlea Reservoir. Where the land levels out and the track bends left, cut across to a fence on the right and follow it down a gully to The Howe, a homestead at the head of Loganlea Reservoir.

Now follow the "Kirk Road", a well-trodden path across the Pentland Hills, round to the right where it passes through Green Cleugh on its way to Balerno. Just round the bend from The Howe you will come across a small waterfall on the left. Shortly beyond this turn left on to a zigzag path up the valley side, over moorland and on to the rocky summit of Hare Hill (449m/1472ft). Head SSW (205°) down to signpost on Balerno to Nine Mile Burn footpath, climb over stile and follow path back to Red Moss Nature Reserve.

To shorten the walk, from The Howe stay on the "Kirk Road" through Green Cleugh and back to Red Moss (omitting Hare Hill). Save 1.2km/0.7ml.

13.   Black Mount

Ordnance Survey map No: 72
Distance from city centre: 40km/24.8ml
Walking distance: 12.7km/7.9ml
Amount of climbing: 274m/898ft

Not a high climb, but to an outstanding top, and very pleasant walking.

Park car in side road near Elsrickle. NT062440. To get there, go via A702 (Biggar Road) to 4.2km/2.6ml past Dolphinton then turn right along A721. Elsrickle is 2.9km/1.8ml along this road.

Climb up hill in a NE by N direction (37°) to lower top (421m/1380ft). Then NE (47°) to the top of Black Mount (516m/1692ft. TP). Continue in same direction and

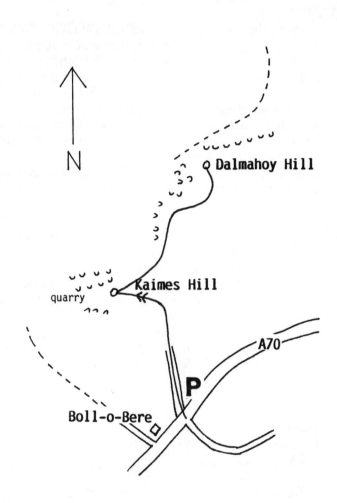

N

Dalmahoy Hill

Kaimes Hill

quarry

A70

P

Boll-o-Bere

WALK 14

descend to col before climbing White Hill (438m/1436ft).

Return by skirting round the NW sides of the hills to the start.

To shorten the walk, return from summit of Black Mount. Save 4.8km/2.9ml.

14. Kaimes Hill and Dalmahoy Hill
Ordnance Survey map No: 65
Distance from city centre: 15.3km/9.5ml
Walking distance: 4.5km/2.7ml
Amount of climbing: 146m/478ft

Though of little height, these hills provide good views of the surrounding country, and are suitable when one wishes an easy day or has little time available.

Park car in farm road off A70 just S of Kaimes Hill. NT135659. To get there, go via A70 to 3.2km/2ml past Balerno turn-off.

Walk up farm road and first of all explore Kaimes Hill (250m/820ft). There is an interesting quarry here. Cross over to Dalmahoy Hill (245m/806ft. TP), taking care at the steep rocky face to its N.

Return by outward route.

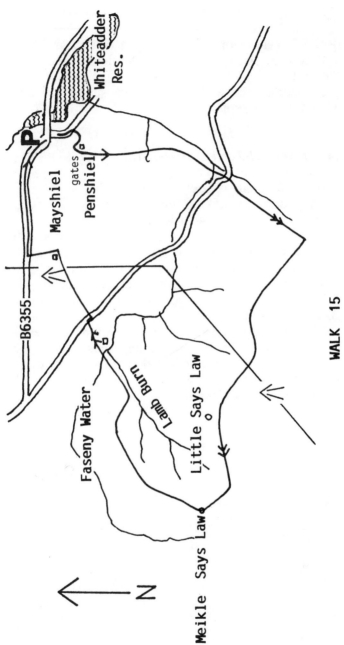

Whiteadder Res.

P

gates

Mayshiel

Penshiel

B6355

Faseny Water

Lamb Burn

Little Says Law

Meikle Says Law

N

WALK 15

LAMMERMUIR HILLS

15. Meikle Says Law
Ordnance Survey map No: 67
Distance from city centre: 48km/30ml
Walking distance: 27.6km/17ml
Amount of climbing: 346m/1134ft

A moorland walk to the highest point in the Lammermuir Hills. The terrain is of wet peat covered with high
tussocks of grass and heather. There are few paths in this
area so walking is strenuous.

Leave car in designated parking area next to cattle grid
on B6355 at the head of Whiteadder Reservoir. NT643642.
To get there, drive E along the A1 to Haddington then S
along the B6369 (signposted "Humbie") for 8.1km/5ml
to a staggered crossroads then E on the B6355, through
Gifford and up on to the Lammermuir Hills.

Walk S past a signpost prohibiting motor vehicles along a
dirt road. Just before a bridge over an inlet of the reservoir
turn right to Penshiel Farm. At the farm go through a gate
on the right then continue S on a farm track, through two
further gates, up the Faseny Water valley to an asphalt road.

Go down the road for about 10yd to two tracks on the
right with a burn in-between. Take the first track and
immediately turn right on a steep path beside a small
gully. Continue diagonally uphill (250°) through heather to
the top of a ridge then go left (218°) following a line of
grouse butts to the highest point.

Navigation from here is difficult because of the lack of paths and prominent topographical features. Meikle Says Law is the highest point on the horizon, 4.5km/2.8ml away to the W (284°). Head towards this along a broad ridge taking care not to lose too much height to either the left or right.

After 2.5km/1.5ml descend into a shallow valley along which run overhead cables and accompanying dirt road. Continuing in a similar direction, climb through heather on the far side of the valley up the side of Little Says Law. Two hundred yards beyond the overhead cables, cross a fence running along the valley and follow a second fence uphill until it makes a left turn on a saddle. To the right is Little Says Law. Go left beside the fence for a further 1.8km/1.1ml to the summit of Meikle Says Law (535m/1754ft. TP).

Head down along a ridge (34°) on an indistinct grassy track for 3km/1.8ml to meet a dirt track at a hairpin bend. Take the higher track down to a river. Cross by a footbridge and continue along the road up a steep incline, past an isolated cottage, to an asphalt road. Cross over and descend on a grassy track, passing beneath electricity cables, to Mayshiel Farm. Turn left over a cattle grid and pass between the farm buildings then on to a road leading to the B6355. Go right along the road for 2km/1.2ml to the starting point.

To shorten the walk, follow the overhead cables NE to Mayshiel Farm. Save 5.2km/3.2ml.

Two cairns on Twin Law : walk 20

Lammermuir Hills from Priestlaw Hill : walk 22

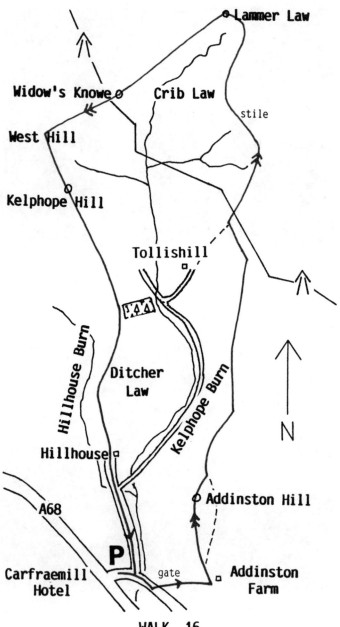

Lammer Law

Widow's Knowe

Crib Law

stile

West Hill

Kelphope Hill

Tollishill

Hillhouse Burn

Ditcher Law

Kelphope Burn

N

Hillhouse

Addinston Hill

A68

P

Carfraemill
Hotel

gate

Addinston
Farm

WALK 16

16. Lammer Law

Ordnance Survey map No: 66
Distance from city centre: 35.7km/22ml
Walking distance: 32.4km/20ml
Amount of climbing: 514m/1685ft

A long ridge walk over the low hills and empty moor-land typical of the Lammermuir Hills culminating in the highest point in the range, Lammer Law.

Park car in considerate spot close to Carfraemill Hotel. NT508534. To get there, drive SE on the A68 through Dalkeith and over Soutra Hill to junction with A697. The hotel is at the junction.

Walk SE along the A697 for 400yd until just beyond petrol garage and adjoining houses. Climb over rusty gate on left and climb diagonally across field to line of trees. Follow these E on infrequently used footpath to Addinston Farm. Here turn left (NNW) on to farm track, right at fork near trees, and up on to the ridge then go NNW to the top of Addinston Hill (383m/1256ft).

Continue along ridge for further 4km/2.4ml until over-head cables are reached. Go left along service road to Tollishill-Longyester pass (gravel track) then right, pass-ing beneath the cables. Continue NE over stile beside gate, round head of Crib Cleugh, pass twin summits of Crib Law and down to broad saddle. (There is a track that departs to the left between the summits of Crib Law and another that goes off to the right. Do not take either of them.) On the saddle the main track bends left. Continue NNE here on muddy track over peat moorland. At highest point cut left through heather to summit of Lammer Law (527m/1728ft. TP. Cairn).

Descend ridge to SW (232°), over Widow's Knowe, then up to join line of trees on top of West Hill (451m/1479ft). Go SSE (150°) over Kelphope Hill then on to a farm track going S along the ridge between Kelphope and Hillhouse Burns, past (or over) Ditcher Law and down to Hillhouse. Follow the asphalt road down the valley to Carfraemill Hotel.

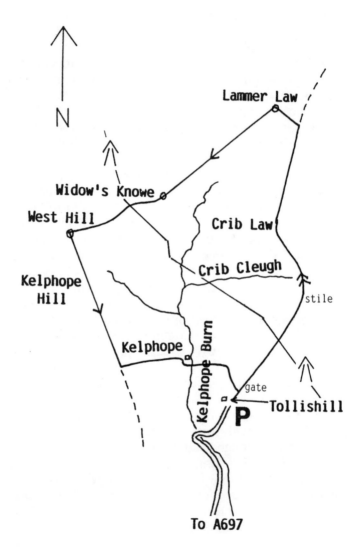

N

Lammer Law

Widow's Knowe

West Hill

Crib Law

Crib Cleugh

stile

Kelphope
Hill

Kelphope

Kelphope Burn

gate

Tollishill

P

To A697

WALK 17

To shorten the walk, from Lammer Law return to Tollishill-Longyester track and follow it S to Tollishill, then take the asphalt road down valley to hotel. Save 2.4km/1.5ml.

17. Head of Kelphope Valley

Ordnance Survey map No: 66
Distance from city centre: 41km/25.2ml
Walking distance 17km/10.6ml
Amount of climbing: 387m/1269ft

A moorland walk to the highest point in the Lammermuir Hills. Lammer Law provides a stunning panoramic view of most of south-east Scotland.

Park at side of road close to Tollishill Farm. NT518579. To get there, drive SE on A68 through Dalkeith and over Soutra Hill to junction with A697. Turn on to A697 then immediately left at Carfraemill Hotel on to unclassified road heading N. At fork go right, then, after a further 3.2km/2ml, take hairpin bend to right just before metal cattle cages. Park at end of surfaced road.

Go through gate and walk NE along gravel track. Just before the overhead cables the track is joined from the right by service road which departs to the left after a few yards. Continue NE on original track passing beneath the cables, over stile beside gate, round the head of Crib Cleugh, close by twin summits of Crib Law and down to broad saddle. (There is a track that departs to the left between the summits of Crib Law and another that goes off to the right. Do not take either of these). On the saddle the main track bends left. Continue NNE here on muddy track over peat moorland. At highest point cut through heather to summit of Lammer Law (527m/1728ft. TP. Cairn).

Descend to ridge to SW (232°), over Widow's Knowe, then up to join line of trees on top of West Hill (451m/1479ft). Go SSE (150°) over Kelphope Hill then

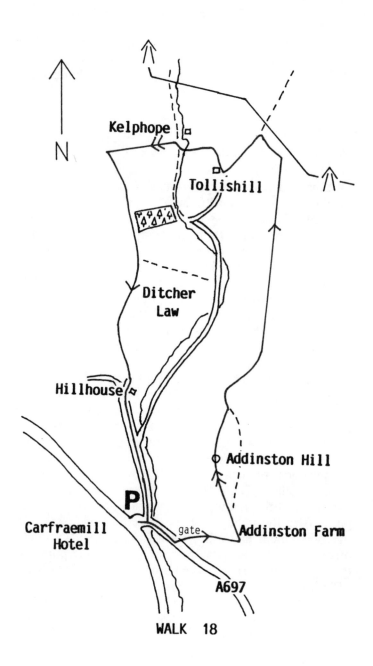

N

Kelphope

Tollishill

Ditcher
Law

Hillhouse

Addinston Hill

P

Carfraemill
Hotel

gate

Addinston Farm

A697

WALK 18

E down to Kelphope Burn and up the far side of the valley to Tollishill.

To shorten the walk, retrace steps from Lammer Law. Save 3.4km/2.1ml.

18. *Tollishill*

Ordnance Survey map No: 66 or 73

Distance from city centre: 35.7km/22ml

Walking distance: 21km/13ml

Amount of climbing: 373m/1223ft

A typical Lammermuir ridge walk with views of endless slopes, low hills and empty moorland.

Park in considerate spot close to Carfraemill Hotel. NT508534. To get there, drive SE on A68 through Dalkeith and over Soutra Hill to junction with A697. Hotel is at junction.

Walk SE along the A697 for about 400yd until just beyond petrol garage and adjoining houses. Climb over rusty gate on left and climb diagonally across field to line of trees. Follow these E on infrequently used footpath to Addinston Farm. Here turn left (NNW) on to farm track, right at fork near trees, and up on to the ridge then go NNW to the top of Addinston Hill (383m/1256ft).

Continue N along ridge for further 4km/2.4ml until overhead cables are reached. Go left along the service road to Tollishill-Longyester pass (gravel track) then left to Tollishill Farm. Turn right just before standing stone and pass to left of large barn. Cross fields at rear and descend to Kelphope. From here climb steeply to W on to ridge then follow it S, along farm track, past (or over) Ditcher Law and down to Hillhouse. Follow asphalt road down valley to Carfraemill Hotel.

To shorten the walk, from Tollishill follow road down valley back to hotel. Save 2.4km/1.4ml.

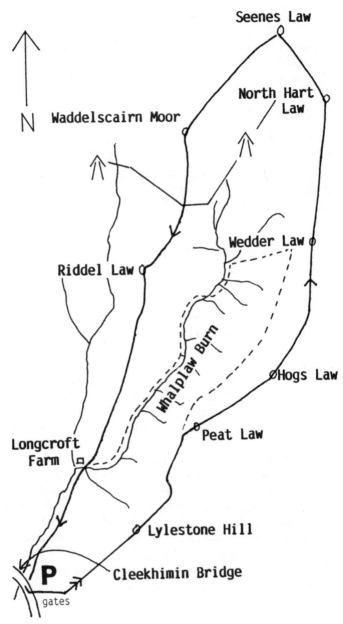

Seenes Law

North Hart
Law

Waddelscairn Moor

Wedder Law

Riddel Law

Whalplaw Burn

Hogs Law

Longcroft
Farm

Peat Law

Lylestone Hill

P

Cleekhimin Bridge

gates

WALK 19

19. Seenes Law
Ordnance Survey map No: 73
Distance from city centre: 37.3km/23ml
Walking distance: 27.3km/17ml
Amount of climbing: 419m/1374ft

A ridge walk, over grazing land and empty moorland.

Park on verge of minor road leading to Longcroft Farm, close to junction with A697. NT522523. To get there, drive SE on A68 through Dalkeith and over Soutra Hill. Turn left on to the A697 at Carfraemill Hotel then, after 1.6km/1ml, left on to minor road at Cleekhimin Bridge.

There is a house on either side of the minor road at Cleekhimin Bridge. The older one used to be the local school. Go on to the main road then climb over the gate next to the new house. Walk along edge of the field, over another gate then up tree-lined gully and on up to top of Lylestone Hill (389m/1275ft). Now follow ridge NE over Peat Law (414m/1357ft) and Hogs Law (448m/1469ft) to Wedder Law (445m/1459ft) then N to North Hart Law then pass beneath overhead cables, swing round the head of Whalplaw Burn and climb W on to Seenes Law (513m/1682ft). There is a faint track of a "Herring Road" along ridge from Lylestone Hill to North Hartlaw over which saut herrin' were once carried from Dunbar to the Border Abbeys.

From Seenes Law head SW (227°) down ridge then S over Waddelscairn Moor (455m/1492ft) and continue S along ridge, back under overhead cables, over Riddel Law and down to Longcroft Farm. Walk along road back to starting point.

To shorten the walk: (1) From Wedder Law head WSW (254°) down to Whalplaw Burn then follow farm track down the valley to Longcroft (save 7.8km/4.8ml). (2) From saddle between Waddelscairn and Riddel Law, head ESE (120°) down to Whalplaw Burn then follow track down the valley to Longcroft. This is no shorter in length, but much easier walking.

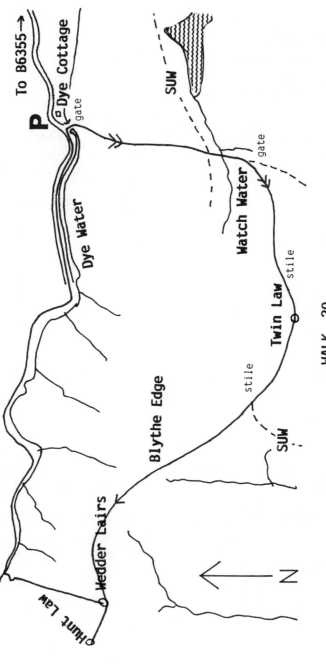

WALK 20

20.   Twin Law

Ordnance Survey map No: 67 or 74
Distance from city centre: 57km/35.3ml
Walking distance: 31.6km/19.5ml
Amount of climbing: 374m/1226ft

A moorland ridge walk incorporating Twin Law on which there are two cairns, each the size of a small tower and in which one can sit and contemplate the view across to the Cheviot Hills in England.

Park on grass beside access road to Dye Cottage. NT649580. To get there, drive SE on A68 (Dalkeith road). At 6.4km/4ml beyond Dalkeith turn left on to A6093 then right at Pencaitland on to B6355. At junction at top of escarpment of Lammermuir Hills, go straight ahead on unclassified road. After a further 9.6km/6ml, turn right (signposted "Dye Cottage"), drive past Horseupcleugh Farm and on to Dye Cottage.

Cross the bridge, go through the gate and follow the farm track over the ridge to Watch Water. Shortly before the river the track is joined by the Southern Upland Way (SUW). Use the footbridge to cross the water then continue along the track to a gate just beyond the trees on the right. Here turn right and follow SUW signs beside fence then over stile at stone wall to Twin Law (447m/1466ft. TP. Two unusual cairns, visitor's book).

Head NW over stile at fence then along summit ridge. In just over 1km/0.6ml, at the start of a gravel road, the SUW departs to the SW. Continue along the ridge, beside the regional boundary fence, over Blythe Edge and Wedder Lairs (486m/1594ft), past Titling Cairn (an erect oblong stone) and on to Hunt Law (495m/1623ft). Last hill before the overhead cables).

Turn back as far as Wedder Lairs then descend ridge N to farm track. (NB: Trying to cut across from Hunt Law leads one into very rough heather and gullies). Walk down the track to Dye Water then follow the farm road down the valley to Dye Cottage.

To shorten the walk, descend N from Blythe Edge. Save 9.7km/6ml.

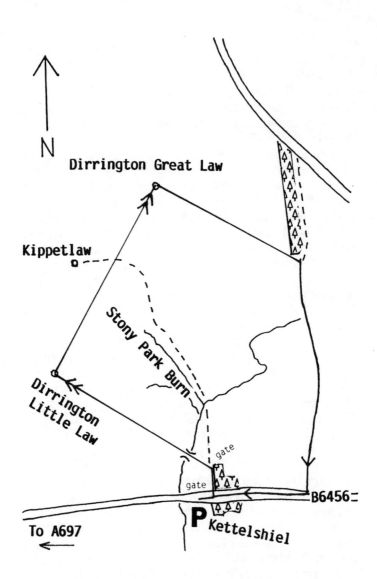

N

Dirrington Great Law

Kippetlaw

Stony Park Burn

Dirrington
Little Law

gate

gate

P Kettelshiel

B6456

To A697

WALK 21

21.   Dirrington Laws
Ordnance Survey map No: 67
Distance from city centre: 59.6km/37.1ml
Walking distance: 14.5km/8.8ml
Amount of climbing: 314m/1029ft

A pair of rounded hills on the southern edge of the Lammermuir Hills that stand out from the surrounding low-level countryside.

Park on verge of B6456 just W of Kettelshiel. NT703518. To get there, take the A68 over Soutra Hill to Carfraemill then the A697. At 13.6km/8.5ml beyond Carfraemill Hotel turn left on to the B6456 for a further 11.2km/7ml to Kettelshiel.

Go through gate and head NNW beside edge of woods, through a second gate then straight ahead on path to a footbridge. Cross over then cut uphill (302°) through bracken and heather on to Dirrington Little Law (363m/1190ft. Cairn). Descend NE (40°), cross saddle then climb on to Dirrington Great Law (398m/1305ft. TP. Cairns).

Descend ridge to SE to trees then follow path S to road (B6456). Turn right and return to Kettelshiel.

To shorten the walk: (1) Return from Dirrington Little Law. Save 7.3km/4.5ml. (2) Omit Dirrington Little Law by going direct to Dirrington Great Law. Save 1.3km/0.8ml.

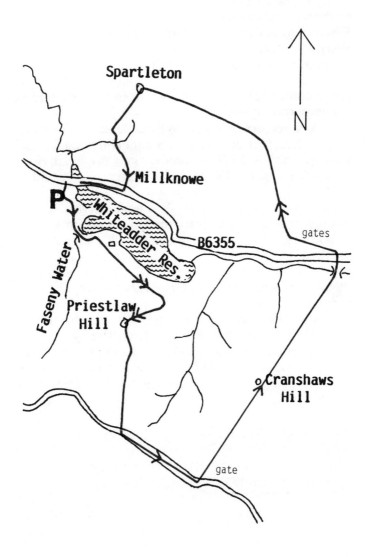

Spartleton

Millknowe

P

Whiteadder Res.

B6355

gates

Faseny Water

Priestlaw
Hill

Cranshaws
Hill

gate

N

WALK   22

22. *Spartleton*

Ordnance Survey map No: 67
Distance from city centre: 48km/30ml
Walking distance: 23.2km/14.5ml
Amount of climbing: 399m/1308ft

A high-level walk around the beautiful Whiteadder Reservoir.

Leave car in designated parking area next to cattle grid on B6355 at the head of Whiteadder Reservoir. NT643642. To get there, drive E along the A1 to Haddington then S along the B6369 (signposted "Humbie") for 8km/5ml to a staggered crossroads at Gifford then E on the B6355 through Gifford and up on to the Lammermuir Hills.

Walk S, past signpost prohibiting motor vehicles, along dirt road, across bridge over Faseny Water, to Priestlaw Farm. Pass through farm and leave on dirt track heading SE then SW. Shortly after bend cut up to right through bracken and heather on to Priestlaw Hill (428m/1403ft. Cairn, remains of stone enclosure). There is a second cairn 50yd N from where a splendid view of the reservoir is obtained.

Head S along ridge then left a little to meet track through heather. Continue S to road. Go left along road for 1.4km/0.9ml to cattle grid then pass through gate on left, climb a little then follow ridge NNE (31°) over Cranshaws Hill and down to river close to St Agnes. Cross bridge to farmhouse and walk up to road (B6355). At cattle grid go through gate and uphill a few yards to another gate. Now go left along edge of field until just above trees then head NNW (340°) up ridge and then to Spartleton (468m/1535ft. TP. Cairn).

Descend SW until grassy track is encountered then follow this left, above gullies, down to Millknowe and road. Go right along road for short distance to starting point.

To shorten the walk, from Priestlaw Hill turn back and go NNE over Friar's Nose and bridge over river to road. On far side follow track above trees up on ridge leading up to Spartleton. Save 9km/5.5ml.

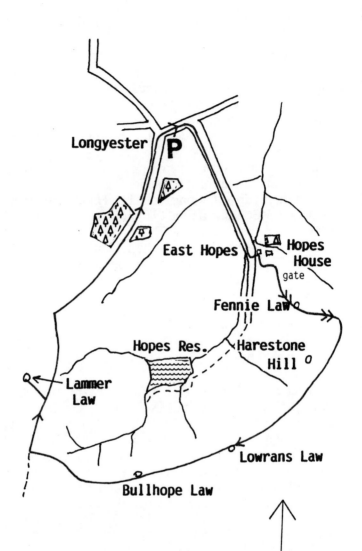

Longyester

P

East Hopes

Hopes House

gate

Fennie Law

Hopes Res.

Harestone Hill

Lammer Law

Lowrans Law

Bullhope Law

N

WALK 23

23. Hope Hills

Ordnance Survey map Nos: 66 and 67
Distance from city centre: 40km/24.5ml
Walking distance: 22.6km/14ml
Amount of climbing: 287m/941ft

A circular moorland ridge walk incorporating the highest point in the Lammermuir Hills, Lammer Law, which provides a superb panoramic view across East Lothian.

Park at Longyester. NT545652. To get there, drive SE on A68. At 6.4km/4ml beyond Dalkeith turn left on to A6093 then right at Pencaitland on to B6355. On western outskirts of Gifford turn right on unclassified road signposted "Longyester" and park, without creating an obstruction, in road bearing "no through road" sign.

Head NE along road then next right to East Hopes. Cross bridge and pass private entrance to Hopes House then go left on track through woodlands that leads to field behind cottage. Climb over gate into grazing land and head SE (134°) climbing steeply over Fennie Law then up the escarpment on to ridge.

Go SW along heather-covered ridge over Lowrans Law (497m/1630ft), then, still on ridge, gradually swing round to W until fence and gravel track is met descending from Crib Law. Follow this NNE. Where the main track bends left, continue straight ahead on muddy track over peat moorland. At highest point cut left through heather to summit of Lammer Law (527m/1728ft. TP. Cairn).

Retrace steps to track and continue NNE down to Longyester.

To shorten the walk, cut right from ridge down to Hopes Reservoir then follow track beside Hopes Water back to East Hopes then by road to Longyester. Save 3.9km/2.4ml.

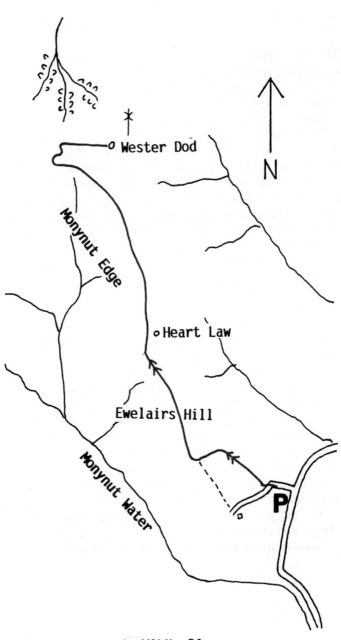

Wester Dod

Monynut Edge

Heart Law

Ewelairs Hill

Monynut Water

N

P

WALK 24

24. *Monynut Edge to Wester Dod*

Ordnance Survey map No: 67

Distance from city centre: 65.7km/41ml

Walking distance: 13.8km/8.5ml

Amount of climbing: 130m/426ft

An easy walk on the eastern end of the Lammermuir Ridge. Being the highest ground before the North Sea, there are superb views across the Firth of Forth to Fife, out to sea, and S to the distant twin peaks of the Eildon Hills with the Cheviots beyond.

Park on grass near access road to Middle Monynut Farm. NT728562. To get there, drive along the A1. Turn right just beyond Cockburnspath on to minor road (signposted "Abbey St Bathans"). At fork go right (signposted "Monynut"). The farm is on the brow of a hill just beyond a ford.

Walk along the farm road a short distance then go up edge of gully on right. Cut across head of gully to red shed then head NNW along grass track. Follow this track along the Monynut Edge, over Ewelairs Hill and Heart Law (391m/1282ft), to the bottom of Wester Dod. Here the path passes a gate on the right then runs alongside a fence. The TP is clearly visible on the summit of Wester Dod but heading directly towards it would entail crossing heather and possibly disturbing nesting birds. Continue along track until at head of gully on left. At this point, go right, across fence, uphill 10 paces then left on deeply cut path through heather. When it is possible to see ahead to a radio mast and the entire hill on which it stands, turn right and you will find a grass track that leads up to the TP (410m/1344ft).

Return by following the outward route to start.

It is not practicable to shorten this walk.

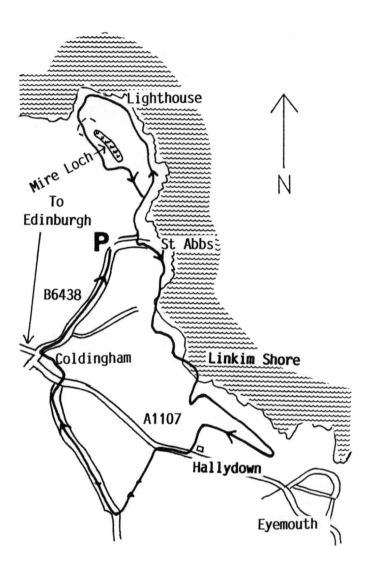

Lighthouse

Mire Loch

To
Edinburgh

P   St Abbs

B6438

Coldingham   Linkim Shore

A1107

Hallydown

Eyemouth

N

WALK   25

25. St Abb's Head

Ordnance Survey map No: 67
Distance from city centre: 75.4km/46.8ml
Walking distance: 26km/16.2ml
Amount of climbing: 404m/1325ft

A stimulating sea cliff walk, often precariously close to edge. There are good paths, superb views and refreshing sea breezes. St Abb's Head is an internationally renowned bird sanctuary.

Park in free carpark beside Nature Reserve Centre and Headstart Coffee Shop just outside the village of St Abbs. NT913674. To get there, take the A1 until just beyond Cockburnspath, then A1107 to Coldingham, then B6438 to St Abbs.

Walk past coffee shop and climb over stile then follow footpath, at first parallel with road then across rolling grassland and cliff tops to St Abb's Head lighthouse. Walk around headland then cross access road where it enters Reserve and head for Mire Loch. Climb over stile and follow path along southern shore to dam wall, jump over outflow channel and rejoin main path back to St Abbs.

At road go left, past church then next right through residential area and over crossroads to end of road at cliff top. Now follow the footpath (signposted) to Coldingham Sands. On far side of bay climb over stile and continue on clifftop path to Eyemouth. Note that at Linkim Shore bay the route crosses the sand then heads inland a little up a valley before regaining clifftop.

On reaching outskirts of Eyemouth cut across to corner of housing estate on right then turn right again to head back towards St Abbs on path then dirt track across fields. After 1km/0.6ml follow track left to Hallydown Farm and main road (A1107).

Walk right along the road, past some cottages, then down to bend over burn and turn left on to dirt track. At end go through gate, follow hedge on right across grazing land, then join another farm track over brow of hill

(114m/374ft. TP) and down to quiet country lane. Follow this NE for 2km/1.2ml to A1107. Here go right for a few paces then left down the lane and left again on to footpath behind houses. Cross bridge over burn and turn left along road to centre of Coldingham then follow St Abbs road back to carpark.

To shorten the walk: (1) Omit St Abb's Head section of the walk (the most interesting part). Save 8.1km/5ml. (2) Omit St Abbs to Eyemouth section. Reduces walk to only 7.5km/4.6ml. (3) Follow A1107 from Hallydown to Coldingham. This saves about 1km/0.6ml but entails a dangerous walk along a busy road with no edges for pedestrians.

Gladhouse Reservoir from Moorfoot Hills : walk 27

Gladhouse Reservoir and Pentland Hills from Moorfoot Hills : walk 27

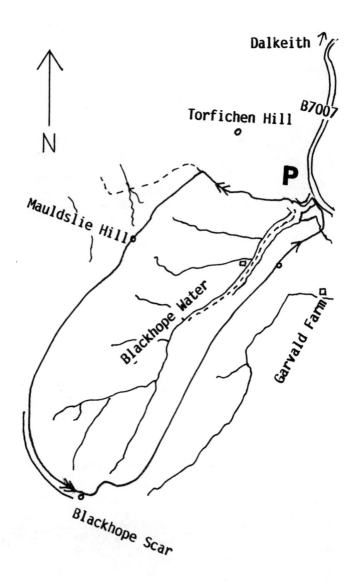

Dalkeith

B7007

Torfichen Hill

P

Mauldslie Hill

Blackhope Water

Garvald Farm

Blackhope Scar

WALK 26

MOORFOOT HILLS

26. Blackhope Scar
Ordnance Survey map No: 73
Distance from city centre: 29km/18ml
Walking distance: 20km/12.4ml
Amount of climbing: 345m/1131ft

An arduous but rewarding walk to the highest point in Midlothian. There are very few paths on the high ground.

Park car on grass embankment of B7007 close to Blackhope Farm road. NT348524. To get there, drive S on A7. When 11km/7ml beyond Dalkeith/Eskbank turn right on to B7007, signposted "Innerleithen". After left turn into mountains and a cutting (7km/4.3ml), the farm road is on the right.

Walk along farm road. In about 400yd, at hairpin bend, move on to footpath and gradually climb the valley ahead to the saddle between Torfichen Hill and Mauldslie Hill. Climb Mauldslie Hill, then follow a fence along a ridge, gradually bending round to the left, for 5km/3ml to the summit of Blackhope Scar (651m/2135ft. TP). On final ascent there is a path to the left of the fence which bypasses many of the deep gullies.

The return is along another ridge running parallel to, and slightly lower than, the first. Again the way is marked by a fence. Leave by the E beside the fence. After about

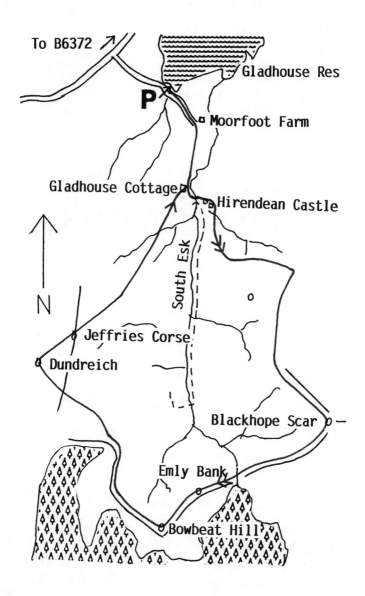

To B6372

Gladhouse Res

P

Moorfoot Farm

Gladhouse Cottage

Hirendean Castle

South Esk

N

Jeffries Corse

Dundreich

Blackhope Scar

Emly Bank

Bowbeat Hill

WALK 27

200yd deviate to the left down one of the gullies until the ground begins to drop away precipitously for a splendid view of the Blackhope valley.

Cut across the ridges of heather and boggy gullies to rejoin the fence. There is one small hill at the end of the ridge. Do not follow the track on the right down the gully to Garvald Farm but stay with the fence over top of this final hill and down the far side to the river (Blackhope Water). Here leave the fence at last. Ford the river, follow it upstream a short distance, then climb the gully ahead to the main road and waiting car.

It is not practicable to shorten this walk, other than by returning before reaching Blackhope Scar.

27. Source of South Esk
Ordnance Survey map No: 73
Distance from city centre: 25km/15.6ml
Walking distance:25km/15.4ml
Amount of climbing: 556m/1823ft

This walk follows a horseshoe route around head of the South Esk valley. Heather, peat bogs, and few paths make the going very rough.

Park car on grassy area off the access road to Moorfoot Farm, next to Gladhouse Reservoir. NT292528. To get there, drive S along A701 towards Penicuik. At 1km/0.65ml beyond the roundabout where the A703 joins, bear left on to the B7026. Pass through Auchendinny then, in 3.5km/2.2ml, turn left on to B6372 (signposted "Temple"). Where the road turns 90° left, go right. Shortly beyond the turn-off to Gladhouse, turn left on to the Moorfoot Farm access road and park on the left when you reach the reservoir.

Walk along road to Moorfoot Farm. Pass house on right then turn right on to another road. After 1km/0.6ml, pass Gladhouse Cottage, cross the bridge over the South Esk then climb grassy embankment to Hirendean Castle (ruins). Follow track up a little then down to gate beside tributary of the South Esk. Go through the gate, pass a

Dundreich : walk 27

Peebles, Glentress Forest and Dunslair Heights : walk 31

sheep pen, then continue on the path, climbing steeply in a SSE (162°) direction to the heather. Follow the path gradually round to the E, past some grouse butts, until you reach a fence along the main ridge. Follow this heading S then SE for 2.5km/1.5ml to the summit of Blackhope Scar (651m/2135ft. TP). Note that on final ascent to summit there is a path to the right of the fence which avoids many of the deep gullies in this region.

Step over fence next to the TP and head towards distant radio mast on Dunslair Heights SSW (208°) on a thin path to right of fence. After about 150yd bear right (247°) with the fence, descend to saddle then climb over Emly Bank then the slightly higher Bowbeat Hill (625m/2050ft). Moving round to right (294°), still with the fence, descend to saddle between the headwaters of South Esk and Leithen Water. Here there is a gate leading to a forestry road. Continue beside fence (344°) until it turns sharp left and begins to descend steeply. Leave fence here and strike out across heather in a NW (324°) direction over brow of hill then down to another fence in shallow gully. Cross this fence and head uphill over rough grassland to Dundreich (622m/2040ft. TP).

Close to the pillar is a fence. Follow it over to the adjacent hill (Jeffries Corse) then, leaving the fence, descend in a NE (44°) direction. Do not follow the more prominent path to the N. Soon Hirendean Castle will come into view in the valley directly ahead. Take steeply descending path down to Gladhouse Cottage then road back to Moorfoot Farm and on to starting point.

It is not practicable to shorten this walk.

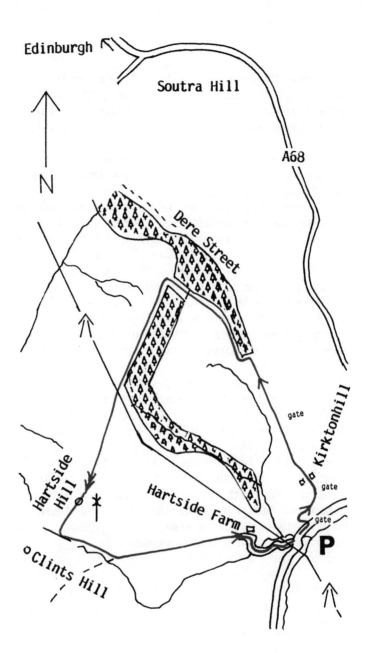

Edinburgh

Soutra Hill

N

A68

Dere Street

Kirktonhill

gate

gate

Hartside Hill

Hartside Farm

gate

P

Clints Hill

WALK 28

28.   Hartside Hill
Ordnance Survey map No: 73
Distance from city centre: 36.2km/22.3ml
Walking distance: 15km/9.3ml
Amount of climbing: 224m/734ft

This is a moderate hill walk over a variety of terrain without any steep ascents or descents. It is reasonably easy going except across the peat bog between the forest and Hartside Hill. This is covered in heather, very wet and has no path across it. There are also numerous drainage ditches presumably for forestation.

Park car at junction with Hartside Farm access road. The road crosses a stream at this point then the track of a dismantled railway. There is a green shack on the right. Do not obstruct this narrow road nor park in a passing place. NT475538. To get there, drive S on the A68 (Lauder road) for 35km/22ml. Take the first road to the right 6.8km/4.2ml past Soutra Hill and follow the signs for Hartside.

Walk back along the road for a few paces to a gate on the left. Go through the gate and climb the embankment then head NE (30°) across grazing land to another gate and a line of trees. Use the gates as all the fences in this region are electrified. Follow the trees to some farm buildings and cottages (Kirktonhill) and leave via a gravel track beside a cottage and pine trees. Beyond the trees follow a farm track across grazing land heading N over the brow of a hill then pass through another gate and head uphill beside a stone wall. A sign here indicates that this is part of Dere Street, a Roman road.

On reaching a spur of a pine forest go left past a hut then NW along the edge of the forest. Where more trees appear on the left step over the fence and continue straight ahead through a gap in the forest. At open ground turn left (SSW 206°) to the end of the tree line (1.2km/0.8ml) then continue directly ahead across boggy moorland, passing beneath an electricity transmission line, and up to the TP and radio mast on the summit of

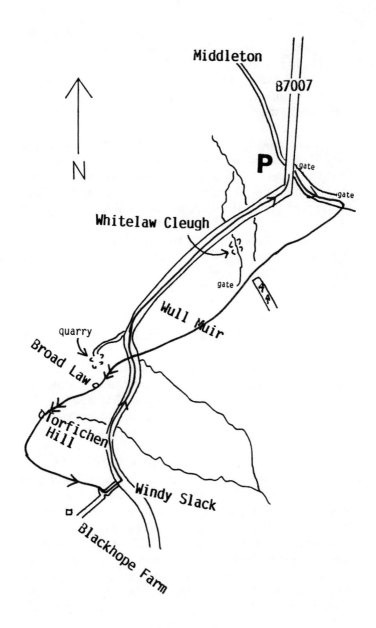

Middleton

B7007

P

gate

gate

Whitelaw Cleugh

gate

Wull Muir

quarry

Broad Law

Morfichen Hill

Windy Slack

Blackhope Farm

WALK 29

Hartside Hill (468m/1535ft). NB: By staying close to the new plantation of trees on the right it is possible to avoid most of the wetter parts of the bog.

From the mast descend about 30ft down a track to a dirt road, cross over and walk down through the heather to a fence and stone wall that runs across the saddle between Hartside Hill and Clints Hill (SW, 233° from Hartside Hill). Follow the wall down (SE) to a gate into grazing land then take the track across the grazing land to a gravel road. This leads down to Hartside Farm. At the farm go right past the main house then down the road to the starting point.

To shorten this walk, at the point where you leave the forest to cross the bog, turn left and follow the electricity lines down to Hartside Farm. Save 3km/1.8ml.

29. *Moorfoot Escarpment*
Ordnance Survey map No: 73
Distance from city centre: 23.3km/14.5ml
Walking distance: 20.8km/12.7ml
Amount of climbing: 303m/993ft

A moderate walk over grazing land and grass tussocks along the edge of the escarpment of the Moorfoot Hills. Superb views over the Firth of Forth and Midlothian throughout the route.

Park car on gravel lay-by near junction of B7007 and minor road to Middleton. NT371566. To get there drive S on the A7 (Galashiels road). At 1.6km/1ml beyond North Middleton, turn right on to the B7007 signposted "Innerleithen". Park on the left at the end of the straight stretch of road near the signpost for Middleton.

Go through a metal gate opposite the road from Middleton and take a gravel track uphill to a second metal gate. Turn right (230°) and follow a low stone wall over grazing land up on to the escarpment ridge. Pass a line of trees on the left and continue to a deep gully (Whitelaw Cleugh). On the far side of the gully go through a small gate and follow a fence SW (228°) then later another stone wall

Forest track, Minch Moor : walk 37

Summit of Minch Moor : walk 37

across rough grassland. This will take you past a young conifer plantation on the left, over the rounded top of Wull Muir then down, over a fence, and on to the B7007 where it enters the range of hills.

Cross the road and the fence on the far side and follow an ascending fence up over Broad Law. There is a small mast near the top and a quarry on the N side. Below, to the E, is Gladhouse Reservoir. Descend a little then, still following the fence, climb to the summit of Torfichen Hill (460m/1508ft. TP).

Descend in a SW direction to join the Gladhouse to Windy Slack footpath where it passes over the saddle between Torfichen and Mauldslie Hills. Go ESE (122°) along the footpath then the Blackhope Farm access road to the B7007. Turn left and follow the road through the gap between Broad Law and Wull Muir then gradually down the escarpment to the starting point.

To shorten this walk: (1) Descend along the footpath beside Whitelaw Cleugh to the B7007 then follow the road back to the starting point. Save 14.7km/9.1ml. (2) Omit Broad Law and Torfichen Hill – on reaching the road between Wull Muir and Broad Law, turn right and follow the road back to the starting point. Save 9.3km/5.7ml.

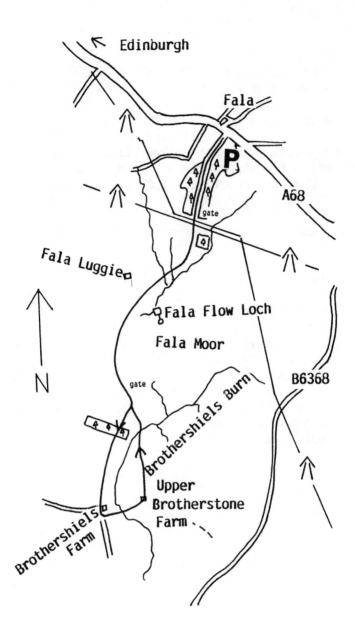

Edinburgh

Fala

P

A68

Fala Luggie

Fala Flow Loch

Fala Moor

N

B6368

gate

Brothershiels Burn

Upper
Brotherstone
Farm

Brothershiels
Farm

WALK 30

30. *Fala Moor*

Ordnance Survey map No: 66
Distance from city centre: 24.7km/15.3ml
Walking distance: 17.2km/10.8ml
Amount of climbing: 174m/570ft

An easy walk on good paths over the bleak expanse of Fala Moor. Many birds of several species may be seen, especially in the vicinity of Fala Flow Loch.

Park car on gravel road off the A68 diagonally opposite the turn-off to Fala. NT437608. To get there, drive SE on the A68 through Dalkeith and Pathhead. At 10yd beyond the signpost for the village of Fala, turn right on to a gravel road through a conifer plantation.

Walk along the gravel road to the end of the forest. Go through a gate and take the track beneath the power lines across the moor, passing Fala Flow Loch to the left and Fala Luggie (a peel-tower now in ruins), to the right.

On the far side of the moor go through another gate and cross sheep grazing land to a line of trees. Continue along the track through the trees then across more grazing land to Brothershiels Farm. Go past a large barn on the left then turn left and take the path behind a small cottage heading E (89°) over Brothershiels Burn then uphill to Upper Brotherstone Farm. From here take the path heading N (352°) to rejoin the track across Fala Moor and so return to the starting point.

It is not practicable to shorten this walk.

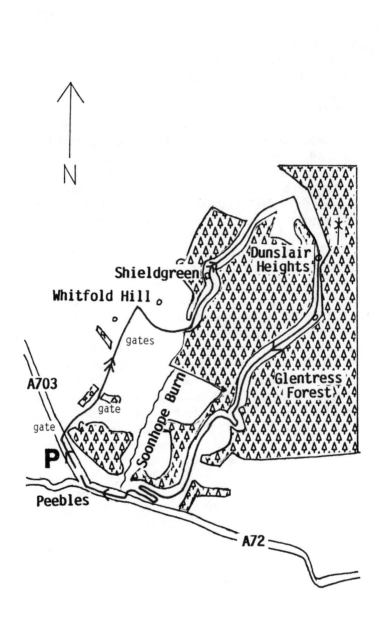

N

Dunslair
Heights

Shieldgreen

Whitfold Hill

gates

A703

Soonhope Burn

gate

Glentress
Forest

gate

P

Peebles

A72

WALK 31

31. *Dunslair Heights*
Ordnance Survey map No: 73
Distance from city centre: 36.2km/22.3ml
Walking distance: 19.2km/11.8ml
Amount of climbing: 478m/1567ft

A delightful walk on good paths through Glentress Forest with a superb panoramic view from Dunslair Heights.

Park in Peebles at carpark on Edinburgh Road 300yd before junction with A72. NT254406. To get there, drive S on A701 then A703 (continuation of same road) to Peebles.

Walk N along Edinburgh Road to house on right at beginning of Ven Law High Road. Go through large black gate adjacent to house and walk up tree-lined track heading NNE (24°), past Venlaw Castle Hotel and out of forest on to open hillside. Continue on grass track round to right past Whitfold Hill, then left at fork and over gate into Glentress Forest. Descend gravel road, cross valley floor (small wooden bridge over Soonhope Burn) and climb up to large white house (Shieldgreen).

Pass below house and take path adjoining outbuilding. Climb steeply through forest, crossing two forestry roads, to top of mountain and end of forest. Go right to radio masts and meteorological station on Dunslair Heights (602m/1974ft).

Head S (174°) beside broken dyke, past another dyke, departing to left into shallow gully, then turn right into forest along muddy track to forestry road. Follow this downhill for 2km/1.2ml to a T-junction, go right for 25yd to another T-junction then straight ahead on to footpath between trees. At clearing follow path round to left. On reaching forestry road go right for 2km/1.2ml to a hairpin bend. Turn off right on to steeply descending path a few paces beyond (not at) the bend. This path emerges on to the road opposite the goods entrance to Peebles Hydro. Go left along the road then right along Innerleithen Road to Edinburgh Road and carpark.

To shorten the walk, take the road from Shieldgreen down the Soonhope Valley to Peebles. Save 8km/5ml.

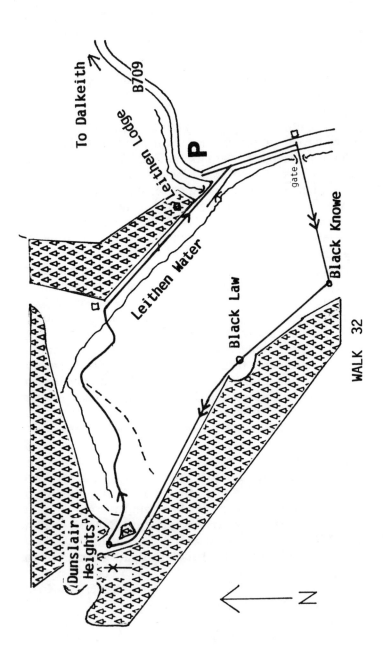

To Dalkeith

B709

Leithen Lodge

P

Leithen Water

gate

Black Knowe

Black Law

Dunslair Heights

WALK 32

N

32. Black Knowe and Black Law
Ordnance Survey map No: 73
Distance from city centre: 40km/24.8ml
Walking distance: 18km/11ml
Amount of climbing: 533m/1748ft

A ridge walk over heather-covered moorland. Reasonable paths.

Use parking area between B709 and Glentress Water about 50yd N of the point where Leithen Water and Glentress Water join. NT329424. To get there, take the A7 then the B7007 (signposted "Innerleithen") just beyond North Middleton and continue S on the B709 to the junction with the access road to Leithen Lodge (signposted "Leithenwater").

Walk S along the B709 for 1km/0.6ml to a farmhouse on the left. Step over the fence opposite and cross the wooden bridge over Leithen Water. Follow fence to gate, pass through and go uphill to the right of a large walled sheep enclosure. Climb up on to the ridge and follow it up on to Black Knowe (521m/1708ft).

Descend in a NW direction (320°) then follow a wall up and over Black Law (538m/1764ft. TP). Continue beside the wall down to a saddle then climb again until a T-junction of stone walls is reached. Here, turn right and continue climbing to the radio masts and meteorological station on Dunslair Heights (602m/1974ft).

Head ESE (122°) down a wide, grass swath through the heather for about 500yd to a track traversing below Dunslair Heights. Follow this to the right, round a tributary of Leithen Water, then downhill, parallel with the burn, into the Leithenwater Valley. Near the bottom swing round to the right then down to join the road along the valley floor. Follow this downstream, past Leithen Lodge, to the junction with the B709 and parked car.

To shorten the walk, cut across to the descending track about 1km/0.6ml before Dunslair Heights, but this misses the best part of the walk and saves only 2.5km/1.5ml.

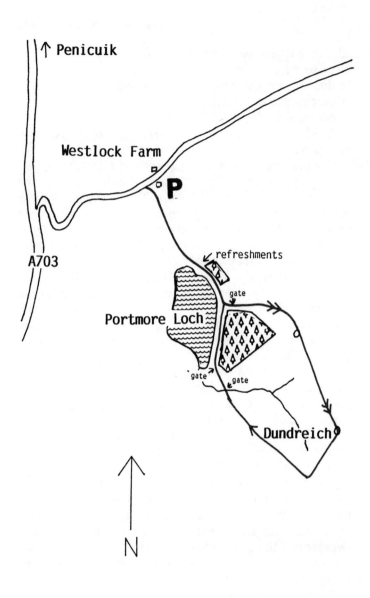

↑ Penicuik

Westlock Farm

P

A703

refreshments

Portmore Loch

gate

gate

gate

Dundreich

N

WALK 33

33. *Dundreich*

Ordnance Survey map No: 73
Distance from city centre: 17km/10.4ml
Walking distance: 11km/6.6ml
Amount of climbing: 357m/1170ft

A pleasant walk around a loch then a climb on to a 2000ft peak. Paths for entire route.

Park in gravel lay-by on minor road at junction with access road to Portmore Loch. NT255514. To get there, drive S on the A701, through Penicuik, to Leadburn then take the A703 (continuation of same road) towards Peebles. At 4.8km/3ml beyond Leadburn turn left on to a minor road signposted "Temple". The access road to Portmore Loch is 1.3km/0.8ml along this road on the right, just before Westloch Farm.

Take the gravel road to the dam wall then walk along the eastern shore to a conifer plantation. Pass through a wooden gate about 100yd before the trees, cut across to the plantation and follow the wall marking its border up on to the brow of a hill. Continue ahead, beside the wall, across a saddle then up on to the summit of Dundreich (622m/2040ft. TP).

Head off SW (216°) along the summit ridge until beyond a steeply descending gully then bear right (298°) along a narrow ridge to a rocky promontory. Descend steeply between crags (303°) to the valley floor and follow a farm track over a burn and through a gate to another gate plus adjacent stile, close to Portmore Loch. Climb over the stile and walk along the track between the forest and the water then along the shore to the dam wall and back along the access road to the starting point. (NB: There is a small wooden hut at the eastern end of the dam that not only sells fishing permits but also canned soft drinks.)

It is not practicable to shorten this walk.

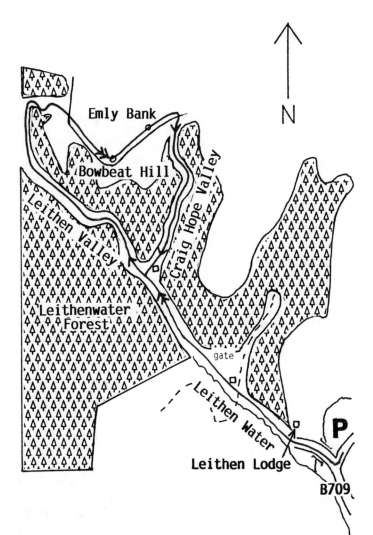

N

Emly Bank

Bowbeat Hill

Leithen Valley

Craig Hope Valley

Leithenwater
Forest

gate

Leithen Water

Leithen Lodge

P

B709

WALK 34

34. Leithenwater Valley

Ordnance Survey map No: 73
Distance from city centre: 40.1km/25.8ml
Walking distance: 23km/14.2ml
Amount of climbing: 424m/1390ft

An easy but long walk through forested mountain glens.

Park beside the B709 close to the confluence of Leithen Water and Glentress Water. NT329424. To get there, drive S on the A7, then turn right on to the B7007 just beyond North Middleton (signposted "Innerleithen"). Continue S on the B709, over-pass, to the access road to Leithen Lodge (signposted "Leithenwater").

Walk along road following Leithen Water upstream, past an old mansion house then a farm. Go through gate into Leithenwater Forest and follow dirt road up the NW valley, to a derelict house (Craighope) at point where several valleys diverge. Continue along forestry road heading NW. At the head of valley the road sweeps around to the right and stops. A track continues a little further around a small gully then disappears into high, wet grass. At this point cut up to the right (123°) between young pine trees then over heather and peat bog to the top of a rounded hill. At the highest point join a fence and, thankfully, a path heading SSE (152°) on to Bowbeat Hill (625m/2050ft. Cairn) overlooking the South Esk Valley.

Head off NE (43°), still beside fence, over the next hill (Emly Bank) and into the gully on the far side. Here climb over the wooden part of the fence and go SSW (202°) along a forestry road. At the first junction turn left, ford a burn, then go up and around headland to another junction. Here go right and follow a forestry road down Craig Hope Valley to Craighope (abandoned house). Cross footbridge over Leithen Water then return by outward route to strating point.

It is not practicable to shorten this walk.

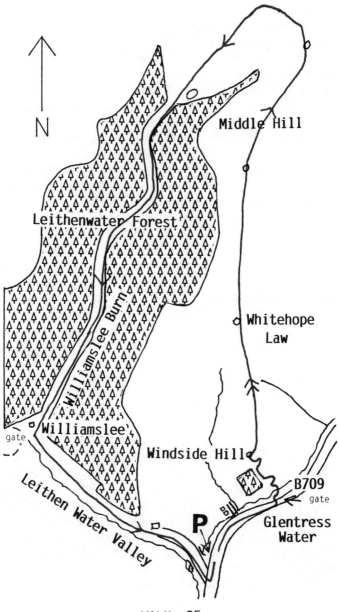

Middle Hill

Leithenwater Forest

Williamslee Burn

Whitehope Law

Williamslee

gate

Windside Hill

B709

gate

Leithen Water Valley

P

Glentress Water

WALK 35

35. *Whitehope Law*
Ordnance Survey map No: 73
Distance from city centre: 40km/24.8ml
Walking distance: 18km/11ml
Amount of climbing: 429m/1407ft

A steep climb up on to, then along, a high moorland ridge with superb views of surrounding hills followed by a pleasant, gradual descent through a deep, forested mountain glen.

Use parking area on B709 about 50yd N of where Leithen Water and Glentress Water join. NT329424. To get there, drive S along the A7. At 1.6km/1ml beyond the village of North Middleton turn right on to the B7007 (signposted "Innerleithen") and continue S along the B709 to the junction with the access road to Leithen Lodge (signposted "Leithenwater").

Walk N along the B709 past Whitehope Farm then past conifer plantation on left (not marked on OS map) to a wooden gate. Climb over, cross grazing land then a footbridge over Glentress Water and climb the steep, zigzag path up on to Windside Hill. From the top, cross the flat area between two gullies then climb up to fence and tiny cairn on summit of Whitehope Law (621m/2036ft).

Follow fence N along summit ridge, descending a little, then climbing again over a rounded hill then bearing round to the left. Where the fence begins to ascend again, go off to the left (218°) across the moor then descend very steeply down a ridge through thinly planted conifer to a circular, walled enclosure, a meeting of streams and the start of a forestry road. Walk along the road beside the water (Williamslee Burn) down the valley to a farm. Here go through a gate then turn left on to farm road down Leithen Water Valley, past an old mansion, to join B709 close to starting point.

To shorten the walk, from the summit of Whitehope Law, descend to the W (280°), enter Leithenwater Forest and take the forestry road right down to the valley

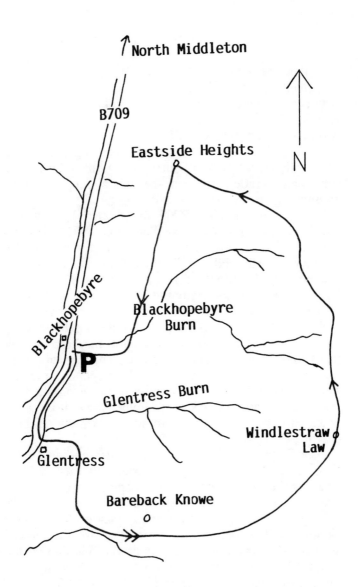

North Middleton

B709

Eastside Heights

N

Blackhopebyre

Blackhopebyre
Burn

P

Glentress Burn

Windlestraw
Law

Glentress

Bareback Knowe

WALK 36

floor then walk out down the valley as above. Save 7.2km/4.4ml.

36. *Windlestraw Law*

Ordnance Survey map No: 73
Distance from city centre: 37.6km/23.4ml
Walking distance: 16.8km/10.3ml
Amount of climbing: 422m/1384ft

This walk traverses the highest ground in the Moorfoot Hills. The summit ridge provides excellent views of the Tweed valley and surrounding hills. The terrain can be very boggy especially in wet weather.

Park in picnic area, a few yards beyond Blackhopebyre, on the E side of the B709. NT344439. To get there, drive S along the A7. At 1.6km/1ml beyond North Middleton turn right on to the B7007 (signposted "Innerleithen") and continue S along the B709 over the pass between Dewar Burn and Glentress Water to the first dwelling on the right.

Walk S along the B709 to the next building, a white farmhouse on the left (Glentress). Just before the farm-house move on to the path to the left above Glentress Burn until beyond the stone wall sheep enclosures. Cross the burn and climb up beside a branch gully opposite (S) on to a ridge, then go left (E), next to a fence, up to the summit ridge. Now head NNE (33°) up to the summit of Windlestraw Law (659m/2161ft. TP).

Gradually descend towards the N then NE, beside a fence, then climb up on to Eastside Heights (593m/1945ft). Finally descend ridge heading SSW (207°) to meet Black-hopebyre Burn next to a stone wall and shelter close to Blackhopebyre and the B709. Cross the burn and follow it downstream to the starting point.

To shorten the walk, from Blackhopebyre ascend to Windlestraw Law via Glentress Rig (save 3.6km/2.2ml). Alternatively, descend Glentress Rig from Windlestraw Law (save 4.5km/2.8ml).

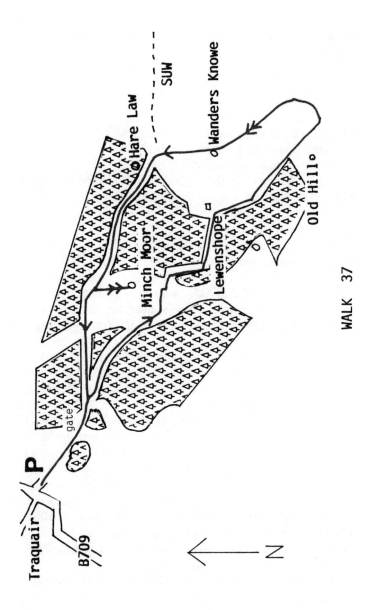

Traquair

P

B709

gate

Minch Moor

Hare Law

SUW

Wanders Knowe

Lewenshope

Old Hill

N

WALK 37

MINCHMOOR AND EILDON HILLS

37. Minch Moor
Ordnance Survey map No: 73
Distance from city centre: 48km/29.6ml
Walking distance: 24km/14.7ml
Amount of climbing: 667m/2187ft

This is really two, close but slightly different, crossings of the hills between the Tweed and the Yarrow valleys. It includes forest and moorland. Part of the route follows the Southern Upland Way (SUW), marked by posts bearing yellow arrows and white insignia.

Leave vehicle in carpark of village hall, Traquair. NT331346. Note, there is a route map of the SUW on the wall of the hall. To get there, take A701 then A703 (continuation of same road) to Peebles, turn left on to A72 to Innerleithen then right on to B709 (signposted "Yarrow"). At Traquair turn left on to minor road opposite war memorial. The hall is a few yards along to the left.

Walk SE along the road following the SUW. At bend to right go straight ahead on dirt track, signposted "Minchmoor", through gate into forest, then, after passing clearing on right, cross forestry road on to footpath through trees. After about 40yd, at a white post, leave the SUW by going right on another footpath. Stay on this path through the forest, going straight ahead when crossed by other paths, firebreaks and road, and following several more white posts, for 2km/1.2ml to stone wall that marks

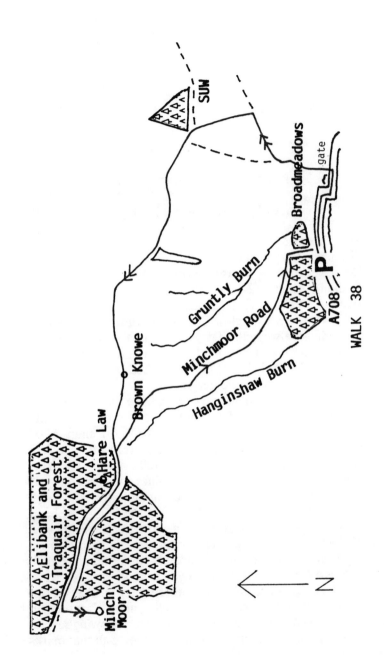

SUW

Broadmeadows

gate

Gruntly Burn

Minchmoor Road

Hanginshaw Burn

P

A708

WALK 38

Brown Knowe

Hare Law

Elibank and
Traquair Forest

Minch Moor

N

the District Boundary. Note that, because of recent tree planting, the path runs to N of that marked on OS map. Go through gap in wall a little downhill (marked by white post), along grassy track to T-junction then right, above head of gully, to cairn beside white post. Here go left down a firebreak then round to right of old stone wall enclosure to leave forest and reach valley bottom near a shepherd's cottage (Lewenshope).

Follow valley down until beyond forest on right and alongside Old Hill. Now climb up through bracken on left to cairn on top of ridge then follow ridge NW over Wanders Knowe (492m/1613ft) to saddle close to edge of forest. Here join the SUW heading E over Hare Law to highest point on northern shoulder of Minch Moor then go left on path through heather to summit (567m/1859ft. TP. Large cairn, splendid views). Retrace steps to SUW and follow it through forest down to Traquair.

For a considerably shorter walk (11.7km/7ml), turn left at District Boundary wall and climb over Minch Moor to join the SUW.

38. Brown Knowe
Ordnance Survey map No: 73
Distance from city centre: 65.6km/40.6ml
Walking distance: 19.2km/11.8ml
Amount of climbing: 377m/1236ft

A gentle ridge walk above the Yarrow valley following part of the Southern Upland Way plus the option of climbing Minch Moor.

Leave vehicle in parking area on south side of A708, next to telephone box, at Broadmeadows. NT408300. To get there, take A7 towards Galashiels. When 6km/3.7ml beyond Stow turn right on B710, cross A72 at Clovenfords and on reaching A707 go left. On the outskirts of Selkirk continue ahead on A708, signposted "Moffat", for 6.4km/4ml to Broadmeadows.

Walk E along A798 for 1km/0.6ml, crossing the river

twice. Just beyond second bridge, at signpost indicating footpath to Galashiels, turn right through gate and follow track uphill beside tree-lined gully. Shortly after passing a side gully on right but before end of trees, turn right on to a steeply ascending dirt track up to top of ridge overlooking the Yarrow valley. Go left (NNW) along ridge to corner and there join the SUW, marked by brown posts bearing yellow arrows and white insignia, WNW along continuation of ridge for 3.8km/2.3ml to Brown Knowe (542m/1718ft). This part of the SUW follows a centuries-old Drove Road once used to drive cattle south from Peebles to markets across the border in England.

Continue along the SUW on to a saddle where the Way crosses gate and enters Elibank and Traquair forest. [Here there is the option of an easy detour (additional 5km/3.1ml) to climb Minch Moor. To do so, continue along SUW over Hare Law to highest point on a shoulder of Minch Moor then go left on path through heather to summit (576m/1889ft. TP. Large cairn, splendid views). Retrace steps to saddle.] From saddle head ESE (117°), traverse SW side of Brown Knowe, on track known as the Minchmoor Road, down ridge then through trees and past group of houses to the A708 and starting point.

To shorten the walk, turn left at col before Brown Knowe and follow path down gully to Broadmeadows. Save 5.7km/3.5ml.

Mid Hill : walk 40

Eildon Hills from Mid Hill : walk 40

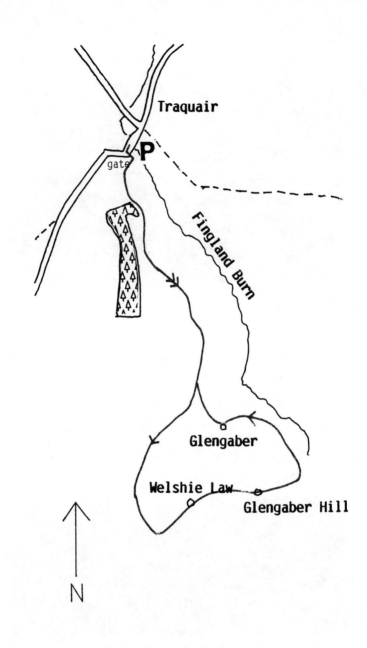

Traquair

P

gate

Fingland Burn

Glengaber

Welshie Law

Glengaber Hill

N

WALK 39

39. *Glengaber*

Ordnance Survey map No: 73

Distance from city centre: 48km/29.6ml

Walking distance: 21km/13ml

Amount of climbing: 406m/1331ft

A moderate walk, mainly along jeep tracks, into a remote part of this sheep country.

Park on remnant of old road on left just before Fingland Burn, 200yd beyond Traquair. NT329242. To get there, take A701 then A703 (continuation of same road) to Peebles, turn left on to A72 to Innerleithen then right on to B709 (signposted "Yarrow") to Traquair.

Cross Fingland Burn using modern road bridge then go left along farm road. At barn turn right. Go through gate, past front of farmhouse and along stone wall. At the end of wall, about 100yd, the track forks. Bear left here on a jeep track beside another stone wall. Follow the track up right-hand side of valley for 3km/1.8ml to another fork. Here the valley divides into two with Welshie Law and Glengaber Hill directly ahead.

Take the right-hand fork to head of valley then cut up left on to Welshie Law (504m/1653ft). Continue E over to Glengaber Hill (498m/1633ft). From here, to the N, the bald summit of Minch Moor may be seen projecting from the surrounding forest while down the valley to the SE lies Yarrow.

Head E down ridge to saddle then go left along track down beside Black Sike (a burn), past a remote shepherd's cottage (Glengaber), then over Fingland Burn and up side of valley to join track used on way up. Follow this back down to the starting point.

It is not practicable to shorten this walk.

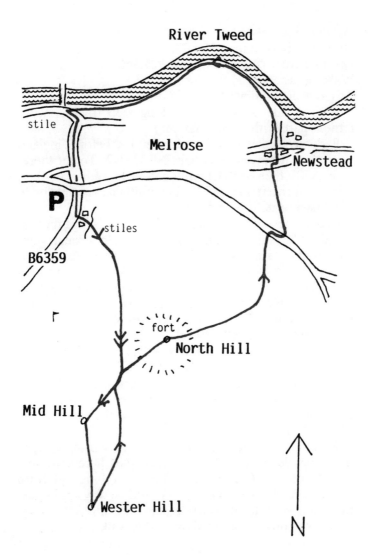

River Tweed

stile

Melrose

Newstead

P

stiles

B6359

fort

North Hill

Mid Hill

Wester Hill

N

WALK 40

40. Eildon Hills

Ordnance Survey map No: 73
Distance from city centre: 63km/39ml
Walking distance: 13km/7.9ml
Amount of climbing: 465m/1525ft

Although relatively short and over low hills, this is a surprisingly good hill walk with many historical sites and superb views. Most of the route follows the signposted, "Eildon Walk" described in detail in the Borders Regional Council's booklet *The Eildon Hills* (cost 50p).

Park at Melrose Railway Station (now a museum). NT546339. To get there, take the A68, then A6091 just before Newton St Boswells to Melrose. The station (signposted) is close to the central Market Square.

Walk S from Market Square along B6539 (signposted "Lilliesleaf"). Pass beneath the new road-bridge then, in 100yd, turn left on to path between houses. Cross burn and climb up flight of wooden steps and stile then head uphill beside hedge, over two more stiles, then along edge of field and over another stile on to open hillside. Follow path through gorse around base of North Hill to saddle between North Hill and Mid Hill. Turn right and climb Mid Hill (422m/1384ft. TP. Viewfinder. Cairn).

Descend steep southern side of Mid Hill and cross over to Wester Hill (371m/1216ft). Return to saddle around base of Mid Hill and climb North Hill (404m/1325ft, site of Iron Age town and Roman lookout post). Descend NE on path through gorse bushes to stile, then down tree-enclosed track to main road. Go right then left down a track. At old railway bridge and T-junction turn right (leave "Eildon Walk") then left down Claymire Lane into Newstead (a village with a 2000 year history). Cross the B6361 and go down Eddy Lane to the River Tweed. Walk upstream, past the "Battery Dyke" to suspension bridge, then go left across field, over stile and S along road into Melrose.

To shorten the walk, omit Wester Hill (save 2.5km/1.5ml) or Mid and Wester Hills (save 3.3km/2ml) or, at railway bridge, follow "Eildon Walk" to Melrose. Save 2.2km/1.3ml.

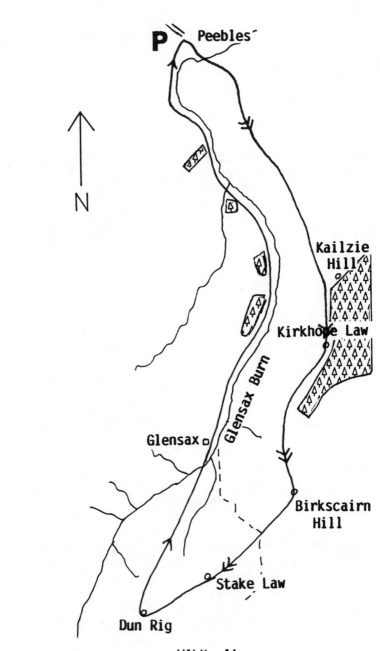

P Peebles

N

Kailzie
Hill

Kirkhope Law

Glensax Burn

Glensax

Birkscairn
Hill

Stake Law

Dun Rig

WALK 41

MANOR HILLS

41. Don Rig from Peebles
Ordnance Survey map No: 73
Distance from city centre: 38.2km/23.7ml
Walking distance: 27.7km/17.2ml
Amount of climbing: 698m/2289ft

A long walk over an established, enthralling route. A "must" for the keen hill walker.

Park car at entrance to Glensax estate in Peebles. NT260392. To get there, drive S on the A701, through Penicuik, to Leadburn then take the A703 (continuation of same road) to Peebles. On entering the town, turn right then left over the bridge crossing the River Tweed. This road turns left and almost immediately there is a road to the right (Springhill Road). Follow this uphill to entrance to estate.

Strike up hill in SE direction along path (being an old drove road which is a right-of-way through to Yarrow as signposted), past Kailzie Hill, over Kirkhope Law (536m/1758ft), to Birkscairn Hill (661m/2169ft). Proceed SW (225°) downhill and at junction of paths continue in this direction up Stake Law (679m/2229ft) (not the lower Stake Law to the S). Continue in same direction to Dun Rig (743m/2433ft. TP). Return by NNE (25°) descending into valley at Glensax, and joining path along Glensax Burn to start.

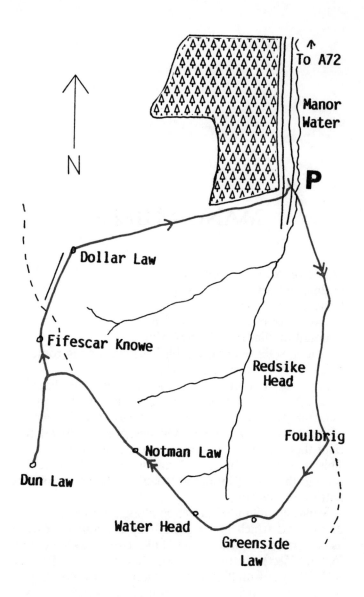

To A72

Manor
Water

P

Dollar Law

Fifescar Knowe

Redsike
Head

Foulbrig

Dun Law

Notman Law

Water Head

Greenside
Law

N

WALK 42

To shorten the walk, after Birkscairn Hill go down track to Glensax (omitting Stake Law and Dun Rig). Save 5.1km/3.1ml.

42. *Dollar Law*

Ordnance Survey map Nos: 72 and 73
Distance from city centre: 53.2km/33ml
Walking distance: 17.5km/10.8ml
Amount of climbing: 611m/2004ft

A six-top round of mountains in this excellent hill-walking country.

Park car at head of Manor Water Valley. NT199287. To get there, go via Biggar Road (A702) to Hillend Park, then Peebles road (A703) to Peebles. At Peebles, turn right (W) on to the A72. After 3.2km/2ml, turn left on to minor road over River Tweed. Follow it on the right, and right again. Do not go on road to left over Manor Water. At T-junction go left and continue S for a further 9.6km/6ml to parking place near end of forest on right.

Cross Manor Water and walk up track on hill in a SSE (160°) direction, round Redsike Head. At Foulbrig strike right up Greenside Law (643m/2111ft), then across to Water Head (613m/2012ft). Now go NW to Notman Law (734m/2409ft). Continue in same direction but when on next ridge turn left and walk along to Dun Law (788m/2585ft).

Return along fine level ridge, but straight to Fifescar Knowe (808m/2650ft) and, following wall, to Dollar Law (817m/2681ft. TP). From that top descend steeply ENE (73°) to start.

To shorten the walk, go direct from Notman Law to Fifescar Knowe (omitting Dun Law). Save 2.8km/1.7ml.

NB: The tops mentioned above which are 2500ft or over are not Corbetts because they are within 500ft of the nearby Cramalt Craig (2723ft).

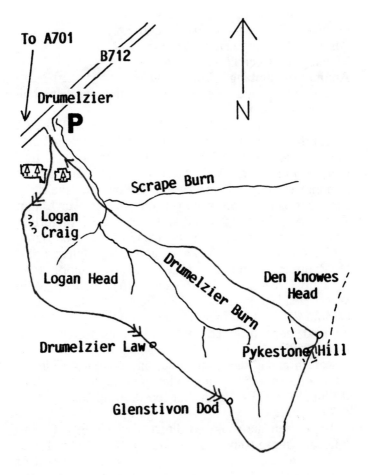

To A701

B712

Drumelzier

P

Scrape Burn

Logan Craig

Logan Head

Drumelzier Burn

Den Knowes Head

Drumelzier Law

Pykestone Hill

Glenstivon Dod

N

WALK 43

43.   Pykestone Hill

Ordnance Survey map No: 72
Distance from city centre: 49.3km/30.4ml
Walking distance: 19km/11.7ml
Amount of climbing: 634m/2079ft

A fairly easy, but still to be respected, walk on the hills.

Park car in Drumelzier Burn side road in Drumelzier (pronounced "Drumeelyer"). NT136339. To get there, take the A702 to Biggar then the B7016 E to join the A701 at Broughton. Go S along the A701 for 2.5km/1.5ml then left on to the B712.

Walk S up hill to Logan Craig, then by Logan Head to Drumelzier Law (668m/2192ft. Cairn). Descend SE (125°) and then up Glenstivon Dod (688m/2257ft). Contour round head of Drumelzier Burn, and head NE (35°) to Pykestone Hill (735m/2414ft. TP. Cairn). Return WNW (300°) by Den Knowes Head, then by road down to the merge of Drumelzier and Scrape Burns. Continue along burn back to start.

To shorten the walk, return from Drumelzier Law by outward route. Save 6.8km/4.2ml.

Looking East from Dun Rig : walks 41 and 47

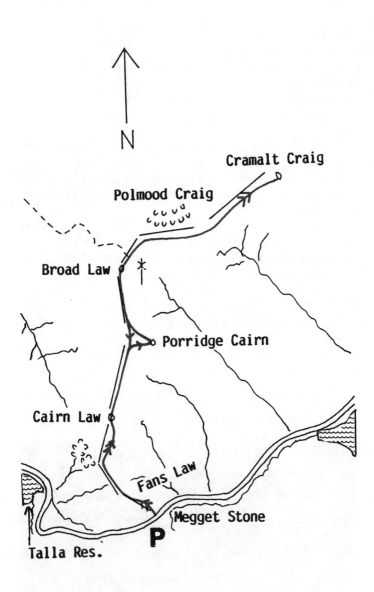

Cramalt Craig

Polmood Craig

Broad Law

Porridge Cairn

Cairn Law

Fans Law

Megget Stone

Talla Res.

P

WALK 44

44.   Broad Law and Cramalt Craig
Ordnance Survey map No: 72
Distance from city centre: 66.6km/41.2ml
Walking distance: 19.3km/12ml
Amount of climbing: 678m/2223ft

A climb to over 2000 feet and a high-level walk in this gentle hill-walking country.

Park car on Talla Reservoir to Megget Water road near Megget Stone. NT151203. To get there, take the A702 to Biggar then the B7016 E to join the A701 at Broughton. Go S along the A701 for 13.5km/8.3ml to Tweedsmuir. Here go right on a minor road past Talla Reservoir to Megget Stone.

Strike uphill, following fence, in NW (325°) direction over Fans Law and on to Cairn Law (717m/2353ft). Continue NNE (14°) then turn on to Porridge Cairn (759m/2489ft). Reverse a little then on to summit of Broad Law (840m/2755ft. TP), the second-highest hill in the south of Scotland and a Corbett. There is an aircraft radio beacon here. Proceed round to other top (830km/2723ft) above Polmood Craig. Descend to E (90°), following fence, and climb Camalt Craig (830m/2723ft. Cairn) – also a Corbett. Return by outward route, but omitting Porridge Cairn.

To shorten the walk, return from Broad Law (omitting Cramalt Craig). Save 7.3km/4.5ml.

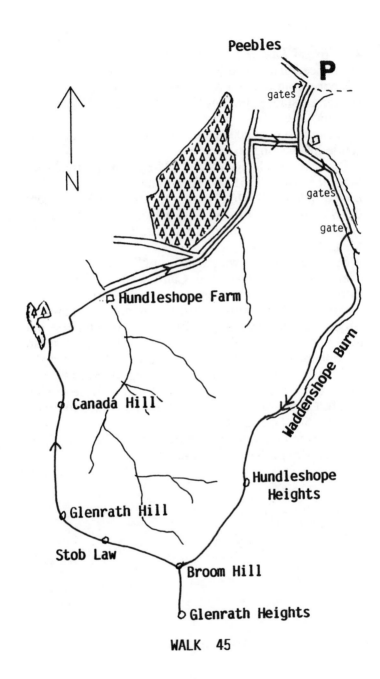

Peebles

P

gates

gates

gate

Hundleshope Farm

Waddenshope Burn

Canada Hill

Hundleshope
Heights

Glenrath Hill

Stob Law

Broom Hill

Glenrath Heights

WALK 45

45.   Hundleshope and Glenrath Heights
Ordnance Survey map No: 73
Distance from city centre: 38.2km/23.7ml
Walking distance: 27.7km/17.2ml
Amount of climbing: 625m/2050ft

A long, circular walk over spectacular, Border hill country.

Park at end of Glen Road, Peebles. NT260392. To get there, take the A701 then A703 (continuation of same road) to Peebles. Go right along High Street and left at small roundabout over Tweed Bridge. Take second right, on bend, Springhill Road, and continue ahead into Glen Road. Pass "no through road" sign and park under trees where asphalt road turns right through a pair of white gates.

Go through the gates and along the asphalt road, past a farm (Haystoun) and stone bridge on left, then along a dirt track beside a burn. Pass a house on right then, 150yd before a small cottage and barn, go through three metal gates on right and follow track round to another gate beside a railway carriage. Go through gate and head SW up gully of Waddenshope Burn. At top continue climbing on to Hundleshope Heights (685m/2246ft. TP). Descend S a little then climb SW up Broom Hill then S on to Glenrath Heights (726m/2381ft).

Return to Broom Hill then descend WNW (290°) to saddle and climb Stob Law (676m/2217ft). Now follow ridge WNW then N over Glenrath Hill to Canada Hill and descend steeply NNW (338°). Just below the summit is the start of a stone wall running in the same direction. Follow this down to and round the right-hand edge of a small woodland as far as a wire fence. Here go right, beside fence, to a small group of trees then left through trees to farm track. Walk along the track, past Hundleshope Farm, to asphalt road. Continue straight ahead along road and take second farm track to right (sign "Bonnington" on nearby tree) to T-junction. Here go left back to starting point.

It is not practicable to shorten this walk.

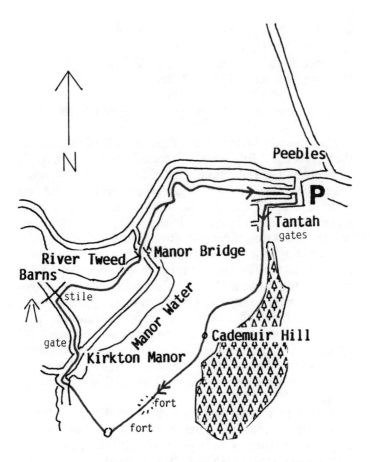

WALK 46

46. Cademuir Hill

Ordnance Survey map No: 73
Distance from city centre: 36.2km/22.3ml
Walking distance: 17.4km/10.6ml
Amount of climbing: 201m/659ft

A scenic walk over low hills close to Peebles, returning along the banks of the Tweed.

Leave vehicle in large carpark on south bank of River Tweed, Peebles. NT251402. To get there, take A701 then A703 (continuation of same road) to Peebles. Go right, along High Street and left at small roundabout over Tweed Bridge.

Walk back to bend just before bridge and continue directly ahead into Caledonian Road. Turn left up Edderston Road and follow it to its end at gatehouse to Tantah House. Pass through iron gate on right and follow path beside wall of Tantah House then over a wooden gate, up valley and along summit ridge to site of ancient encampment (Cademuir Hill). Leave the main path which descends to the left and continue SW along the ridge, past two Iron Age forts (the first being the highest point of ridge, 407m/1334ft), to the last hill of the ridge (NT221370. 318m/1043ft). From here retrace your steps back down to saddle before last hill then descend NW (322°) down gully then alongside stone wall to asphalt road.

Go right along road, across bridge over Manor Water, then right to Kirkton Manor. Just beyond church (on right) turn left, through white gates, and walk along access road to the Barns, as far as overhead cables that cut across the road. Here go over stile on right (sign for "Tweed Walkway") and along grassy track, past trees to River Tweed. Walk downstream to massive, stone "Manor Bridge". Cross river by means of the bridge then continue downstream on north bank to viaduct (old rail bridge) over river. Cross back to south bank and follow through South Park Wood then beside river to Peebles. Alternatively, one could stay on north bank back to Peebles.

It is not practicable to shorten this walk.

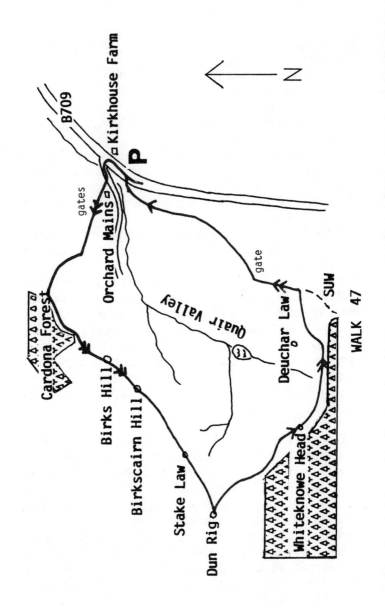

N

B709

Kirkhouse Farm

P

gates

Orchard Mains

Cardona Forest

Birks Hill

Quair Valley

Birkscairn Hill

gate

Deuchar Law

SUW

Stake Law

WALK 47

Dun Rig

Whiteknowe Head

47. Dun Rig from Orchard Mains

Ordnance Survey map No: 73

Distance from city centre: 49.7km/30.6ml

Walking distance: 30km/18.7ml

Amount of climbing: 786m/2578ft

A circular walk around Quair Glen. Includes Dun Rig, the highest of the Manor Hills. There are paths or tracks along both ridges enclosing the glen but the traverse across the head of the glen is over very different terrain.

Park at entrance to Kirkhouse North section of forest on E side of B709. NT318329. To get there, take A701 then A703 (continuation of same road) to Peebles, turn left on to A72 to Innerleithen then right on to B709 (signposted "Yarrow"). After 4km/2.5ml pass Kirkhouse Farm on left. Forest entrance is a further 0.6km/0.4ml along road.

Walk back along road, past Kirkhouse Farm, on to minor road on left signposted "Orchard Mains" and "Glen House". Go round bend, pass entrance to Orchard Mains, then through metal gate on right, across field, through wooden gate, across another field and through another wooden gate, on to moorland. Climb up to trenched area (site of ancient settlement) and along ridge until it descends through bracken and meets track coming up from Quair Valley. Follow this track around Orchard Rig to Cardrona Forest then turn left on path along edge of forest to saddle where a second track from the valley is encountered. Follow this track over Birks Hill and up to fence and cairn on summit of Birkscairn Hill (661m/2168ft). Step over fence and take path SW down across a saddle then up over Stake Law and on to Dun Rig (743m/2437ft. TP).

Descend SE ridge beside fence. Across flat area at bottom runs an old drove road and right-of-way but there remains little sign of it and it is lost completely in the new forestry plantation on the SW side of the fence. Continue beside fence over Whiteknowe Head then left (with fence), along edge of forest, across a saddle and up over southern ridge of Deuchar Law. Just over the top

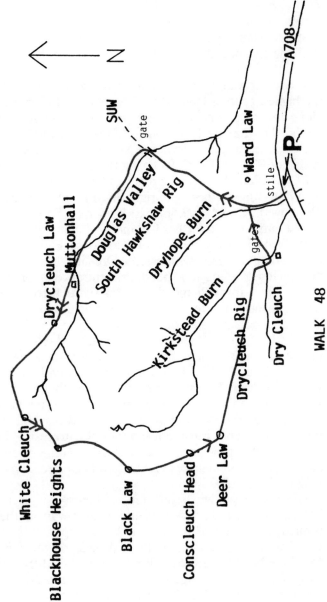

N

WALK 48

White Cleuch
Blackhouse Heights
Black Law
Conscleuch Head
Deer Law
Drycleuch Rig
Dry Cleuch
Drycleuch Law
Muttonhall
Douglas Valley
South Hawkshaw Rig
Kirkstead Burn
Dryhope Burn
SUW
gate
Ward Law
stile
gate
P
A708

climb over gate and follow another fence ENE (72°) for about 200yd, then gradually bear away from fence to right on grass track across to small rounded hill. Over brow of the hill join the Southern Upland Way (marked by posts bearing yellow arrows and white insignia) and follow it down the ridge back to Kirkhouse.

To shorten the walk, it is possible to descend into the glen from a number of points and follow the road to Kirkhouse.

48.   Blackhouse Heights and Black Law
Ordnance Survey map No: 73
Distance from city centre: 63km/39ml
Walking distance: 30km/18.6ml
Amount of climbing: 504m/1653ft

This walk encompasses many of the southern Manor Hills. Although not quite as high as hills to the north, these hills are just as interesting plus there are wonderful views of St Mary's Loch.

Park on verge (as near to fence as possible) on northern side of A708, close to stile of Southern Upland Way, at lower end of St Mary's Loch. NT272243. To get there, take A701 then A703 (continuation of same road) to Peebles, turn left on to A72 to Innerleithen then right on to B709 (signposted "Yarrow"). At Gordon Arms Hotel go right on A708 for 3.5km/2.2ml.

Climb over stile and follow SUW (marked by brown posts bearing yellow arrows and white insignia) between Ward Law and pyramid cairn on South Hawkshaw Rig into the Douglas Valley. Cross footbridge over Douglas Burn and go through gate on to metalled road. Here leave the SUW by going left along road, past farm houses, and up valley for 3km/1.8ml, past the road up Black Cleuch, to a white-walled cottage (Muttonhall).

Take the path behind cottage uphill between saplings, through gap in stone wall, then steeply up through bracken on to Drycleuch Law. Continue climbing NW on to prominent ridge between Dun Rig to right and Blackhouse Heights to left. Go SW along this ridge, following the District Boundary fence, over White Cleuch, to Black-house Heights (675m/2214ft) then on to twin summits of Black Law (696m/2282ft. Cairn).

From the southern summit of Black Law head SSE (168°) over Conscleuch Head to Deer Law then turn E and descend ridge of Drycleuch Rig into Kirkstead Valley. Near the bottom head for the point where the burn coming down Dry Cleuch joins Kirkstead Burn to avoid scree slopes. Ford tributary burn, pass through wooden gate in stone wall and follow grassy track to house (Old Kirk-stead). Exit through gap in wooden fence surrounding homestead and immediately turn left down to the burn, over the footbridge and stile and up embankment to met-alled road. Follow this right for a few paces then turn left on to a dirt road that traverses around base of hill above Dryhope Farm. When road bends left go straight ahead on grass track through bracken until level with tower then cut down to path beside wall and follow it across Dryhope Burn and up on to farm track. Now follow SUW back across fields to starting point.

For a considerably shorter walk, pass small woodland on the left on the way up Douglas Burn then climb up Deepslack Knowe. From the top either head W to rejoin route on Black Law (save 4.2km/2.6ml), or descend SE ridge (Dryhope Rig) to start (save 14.7km/9.1ml).

Manor Hills from Dun Rig : walks 41 and 47

Southern Upland Way ascending Blake Muir : walk 47

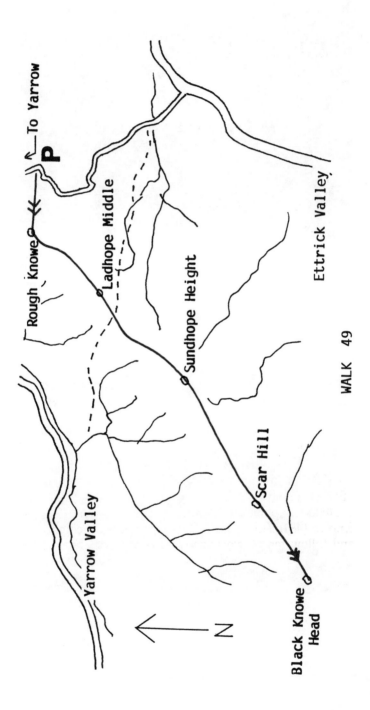

To Yarrow

P

Rough Knowe

Ladhope Middle

Sundhope Height

Yarrow Valley

Scar Hill

Ettrick Valley

Black Knowe Head

WALK 49

N

ETTRICK HILLS

49.   Yarrow/Ettrick Ridge
Ordnance Survey map No: 73
Distance from city centre: 73.7km/45.7ml
Walking distance: 21km/13ml
Amount of climbing: 374m/1226ft

A dramatic ridge walk with steep sides between the valleys of the Yarrow Water and Ettrick Water. Splendid views across both valleys.

Park on grass near cattle grid at top of pass between the Yarrow and Ettrick valleys. NT370259. To get there, take A7 towards Galashiels. When 6km/3.7ml beyond Stow turn right on B710, cross A72 at Clovenfords, and on reaching the A707 go left. On the outskirts of Selkirk continue straight ahead on A708, signposted "Moffat" for 12.8km/8ml to Yarrow. Here turn left, signposted "Ettrick Valley", and climb to top of pass.

Head E, uphill, on right of stone wall to top of Rough Knowe (481m/1577ft). At 90° corner of wall, climb over and follow fence (electrified) on other side. From here the route follows a ridge over heather and rough grassland and past a number of cairns to Black Knowe Head. At first it descends S from Rough Knowe then swings round to the SW and climbs up on to Sundhope Height (513m/1682ft). The route continues SW along the ridge which becomes relatively narrow, climbs over Scar Hill

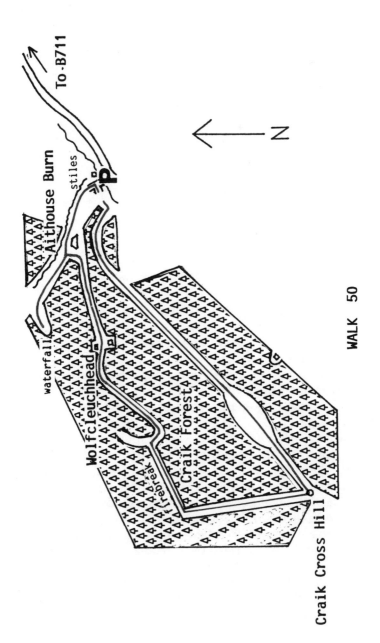

To·B711

Aithouse Burn

stiles

P

N

waterfall

Wolfcleuchhead

firebreak

Craik Forest

Craik Cross Hill

WALK 50

then ascends Black Knowe Head (550m/1804ft. TP).

Unfortunately, one cannot make a circular trip without a long road walk. Therefore, it is necessary to retrace one's steps back to start.

NB: In winter the pass often becomes blocked with snow. If such conditions are prevailing or are imminent, park on left of road just after crossing Yarrow Water, walk up the road a little until just past a small woodland, then go through gate on right and climb Rough Knowe from here.

To shorten the walk, turn back earlier. If parked at bottom of pass one could cut down into the Yarrow valley and follow the river back to Yarrow.

50. *Craik Forest*
Ordnance Survey map No: 79
Distance from city centre: 98.2km/60.9ml
Walking distance: 23km/14.2ml
Amount of climbing: 305m/1000ft

A pleasant forest walk. Follows, in part, a Roman Road that linked a signal station on Craik Cross Hill with a similar station on the Eildon Hills near Melrose (see Walk 40). There is also a signposted forest trail of 5.6km/3.5ml from the carpark to Wolfcleuch waterfall.

Leave vehicle in Craik Forest visitors' carpark. NT348080. To get there, drive S on the A7. Just beyond Hawick, turn right on to B711 (signposted "Roberton") then left at Roberton (signposted "Borthwick Water"). At fork, go right, past "no through road" sign, and continue to entrance to Craik Forest at end of road.

Walk upstream to end of picnic area then go right up firebreak to forestry road and turn left. At fork in road bear left following signpost for Craikhope. Pass open ground to left, then pass sign indicating Roman road and follow road uphill through forest. (The OS map indicates a path parallel and right of forestry road but it is overgrown and virtually impassable). At next fork go right, away from sign for Craikhope. Soon afterwards the road enters wide area free of trees along top of ridge. Along here ran a Roman Road to signal station on Craik Cross Hill. Continue along ridge to end of road then go straight ahead, following path of centurions, to end of forest and wooden gate on Craik Cross Hill (451m/1479ft).

Turn right and head N beside fence (boundary of forest) over rough grass and heather to wooden gate where fence turns left. Now head ENE (64°) through long grass of forest ride to track then follow this in similar direction, past white cottage (Wolfcleuchhead), and take second road to left (opposite a "carpark" sign). From here route follows established forest trail (in reverse).

After 150yd bear right (again opposite a "carpark" sign) and follow path down ride then down wooden steps to Aithouse Burn. Follow path upstream for 1km/0.6ml then left up Wolfcleuch to waterfall. Return by same route (either side of burn) as far as wooden steps. Do not ascend steps, instead continue ahead along path, on to forestry road for 100yd then left back on path, over stile across electric fence, across field and second stile then through new plantation back to carpark.

To shorten the walk, at junction beyond Wolfcleuch-head Cottage, instead of turning left go straight ahead to T-junction then right to carpark, thus omitting Wolfcleuch waterfall. Save 3.3km/2ml.

Annanhead Hill : walk 60

View down Tail Burn from Loch Skeen : walks 61 and 62

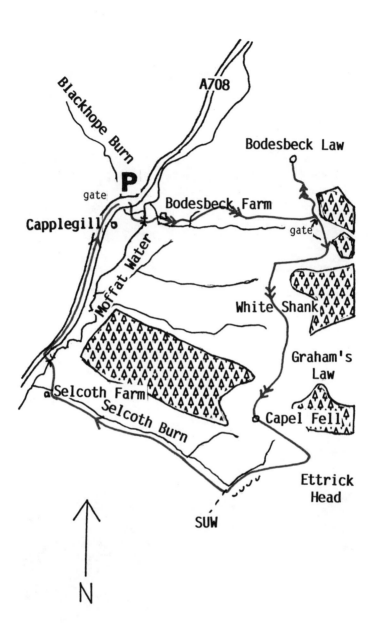

WALK 51

51. Capel Fell

Ordnance Survey map Nos: 78 and 79, or SUW map
Distance from city centre: 90km/56ml
Walking distance: 23.8km/14.7ml
Amount of climbing: 776m/2545ft

A demanding but worthwhile trip up the SE side of Moffat Valley. The crags and scree from Ettrick Head down the Selcoth Burn present a very dramatic mountain landscape.

Leave car in the Moffat Valley just N of Capplegill, next to Blackhope Cottage. NT147098. To get there, take the A701 through Penicuik to Moffat then the A708 (signposted "Selkirk") for 9.3km/5.8ml up the Moffat Valley.

Cross to the S of Blackhope Burn then go through gate on left and along farm road beside burn to Bodesbeck Farm. From farm head E up Bodesbeck gully along track on left of burn to col below Bodesbeck Law. Go over gate in fence (Regional Boundary), turn left and climb zigzag path to summit of Bodesbeck Law (662m/2171ft. TP). This vantage point provides excellent view of Moffat Dale, the Moffat Hills and the Ettrick Hills.

Return to col then follow track to left of fence on to brow of next hill then go W then S, with fence, over White Shank and on to Capel Fell (678m/2223ft). Descend SE, beside fence, to meet the Southern Upland Way at Ettrick Head. Follow the SUW (marked by yellow arrows and white thistle insignia on brown posts) SW down to, and over wooden bridge across, Selcoth Burn then along edge of a deep gully to a stell at a bend in Selcoth Burn. Leave the SUW here and take narrow footpath (later a farm track) down left-hand side of Selcoth Valley to Selcoth Farm in the Moffat Valley. Return along road to Capplegill. Note that shortly after leaving the stell the path crosses 30yd of very steep scree. This requires considerable care.

To shorten the walk, omit Bodesbeck Law. Save 3km/1.8ml.

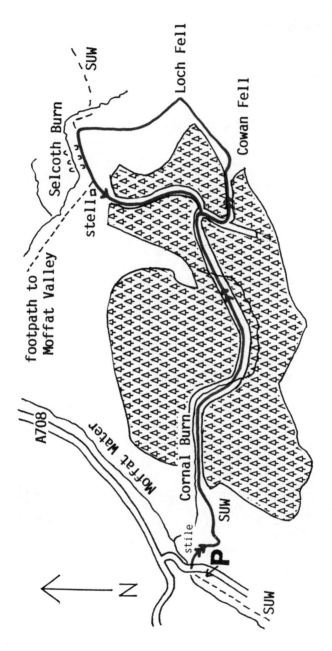

N

A708

Moffat Water

footpath to Moffat Valley

Selcoth Burn

SUW

stile

Loch Fell

Cowan Fell

Cornal Burn

stile

P

SUW

SUW

WALK 52

52.   *Loch Fell from Moffat Dale*

Ordnance Survey map Nos: 78 and 79

Distance from city centre: 85km/52ml

Walking distance: 27.3km/16.9ml

Amount of climbing: 582m/1908ft

Fairly easy going most of the way on forestry roads and mountain footpaths. The crags and scree between Loch Fell and re-entering the forest present a very dramatic mountain landscape.

Park in Moffat Dale. NT107042. To get there, take the A701 through Penicuik to Moffat then the A708 (sign-posted "Selkirk"). After 2.5km/1.5ml turn sharp right on to minor road, cross Moffat Water and park on right-hand verge of road.

Cross the stile on eastern side of bridge and follow Southern Upland Way (marked by yellow arrows and white thistle insignia on brown posts) uphill into forest. After 6.5km/4ml at a right-hand bend, the SUW leaves the forestry road it has been following. Stay with the road, now heading SW, for a further 500yd then turn off to the left on to a narrow, slightly overgrown track between trees, opposite a branch valley. If, while walking along the road, there is a heather-covered hill on the right then you have gone too far. On emerging from forest at end of track, step over fence and follow it left on to summit of Loch Fell (688m/2256ft. TP).

Head NW off the summit, beside fence, for 500yd to a small gully then head due N into deep gully of Selcoth Burn. It is imperative that you head directly towards a rocky gully in the opposite bank. Elsewhere the final descent to the burn is extremely steep and covered in scree. At burn go downstream along path (SUW), past a stell, then alongside Wamphray Burn through forest to rejoin road used on outward route. Follow this back down to the starting point.

It is not practicable to shorten this walk.

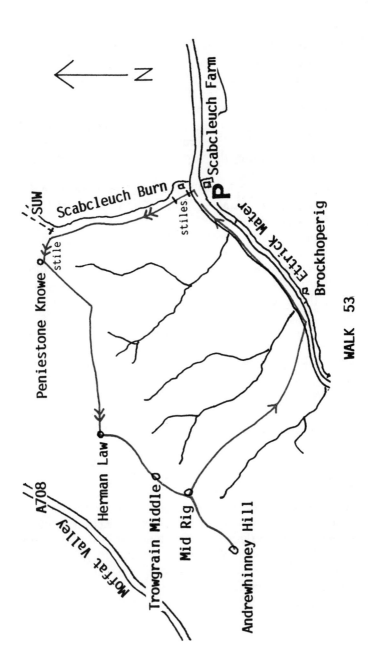

N

SUM

Scabcleuch Burn

stiles

Scabcleuch Farm

P

Ettrick Water

Brockhoperig

Peniestone Knowe

stile

WALK 53

Herman Law

Trowgrain Middle

Mid Rig

Andrewhinney Hill

Moffat Valley

A708

53.   East Ridge of Moffat Dale

Ordnance Survey map No: 79

Distance from city centre: 77km/47.6ml

Walking distance: 20.4km/12.4ml

Amount of climbing: 529m/1753ft

A wonderful high ridge walk between the Moffat and Ettrick Valleys.

Park on verge of Ettrick Valley road just beyond Scabcleuch Farm. NT246143. To get there, go via Peebles to Innerleithen, then S on B709 (signposted "Yarrow"). Cross the A708 at the Gordon Arms Hotel and continue to T-junction. Go right for 5.6km/3.5ml to Ettrick Post Office then right on the single track Ettrick Valley road for 2.4km/1.5ml to Scabcleuch.

Climb over stile opposite Scabcleuch Farm and follow SUW (marked by white thistle insignia on brown posts). At fence at head of Scabcleuch Valley leave the SUW and climb path to left on to Peniestone Knowe (551m/1807ft). Take a few paces NE of summit for a splendid view of St Mary's Loch.

Head SW along ridge beside fence, dropping a little then rising on to a small hill. Here bear right (W), with fence, down across a col then up to Herman Law (614m/2013ft. Cairn). This is the start of an 8km/5ml-long ridge that forms the SE side of Moffat Valley. Follow the ridge (and Regional Boundary fence) over Trowgrain Middle and Mid Rig to Andrewhinney Hill (677m/2220ft. Cairn). Across the Moffat Valley a hanging corrie and waterfall, Grey Mare's Tail, can be seen.

Retrace your steps to Mid Rig then descend narrow SE ridge back into the Ettrick Valley at Brockhoperig. Walk along road to starting point.

Alternatively, should you have a driver to collect walkers at the far end of the Ettrick Valley road (or two parties walking in opposite directions with cars at each end), then the entire ridge may be walked to Bodesbeck Law and the descent made along a forestry road. Additional 2.8km/1.7ml.

It is not practicable to shorten this walk.

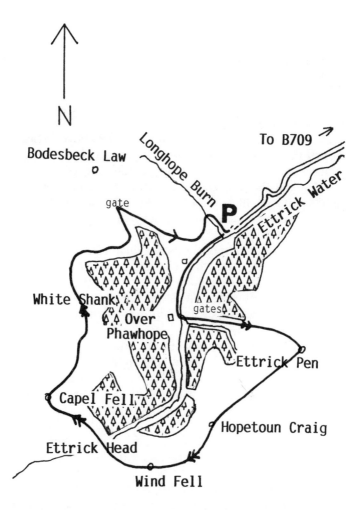

Bodesbeck Law

Longhope Burn

To B709

gate

P

Ettrick Water

White Shank

Over
Phawhope

gates

Ettrick Pen

Capel Fell

Hopetoun Craig

Ettrick Head

Wind Fell

N

WALK 54

54. Ettrick Pen

Ordnance Survey map No: 79
Distance from city centre: 85km/52ml
Walking distance: 20km/12.3ml
Amount of climbing: 658m/2158ft

A trip around the head of the Ettrick Valley including Ettrick Pen, the highest of the Ettrick Hills.

Park at end of road through Ettrick Valley. NT189092. To get there, go via Peebles to Innerleithen then S on B709 (signposted "Yarrow") over mountain pass to the Gordon Arms Hotel. Cross the A708 and go over another pass to a T-junction. Here go right for 5.6km/3.5ml then right at Ettrick Post Office on to the single track Ettrick Valley road.

Walk along the gravel road beside Ettrick Water, past a white house, over a wooden bridge across the river and past Over Phawhope bothy, then bear left on to track that fords then runs alongside Entertrona Burn to forest. Go through gate and immediately go through second gate on left on to forestry road as far as ridge with a fence running up either side of it. Go up the ridge to the top of the forest then continue climbing over rough grassland to summit of Ettrick Pen (692m/2269ft. Cairn).

Follow Regional Boundary fence SW over Hopetoun Craig and Wind Fell to Ettrick Head then NW on to Capel Fell (678m/2223ft) and N over White Shank to col below Bodesbeck Law. At gate on col go right down gravel road beside woodland to stell. Do not take the track that goes to the right here but continue ahead, through gate into forest. Follow the road as it swings round to the left then fords Longhope Burn and descends to asphalt road at parking place.

To shorten the walk, turn right at Ettrick Head, follow the path for a short distance through forest to road then go right along road back to starting point. Save 3.7km/2.2ml.

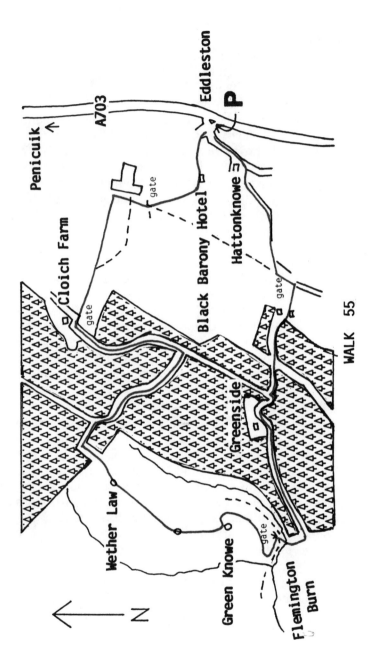

Penicuik

A703

Eddleston

P

Cloich Farm

gate

gate

Black Barony Hotel

Hattonknowe

gate

Wether Law

Greenside

Green Knowe

gate

Flemington Burn

N

WALK 55

CLOICH HILLS AND BROUGHTON HEIGHTS

55.   Wether Law

Ordnance Survey map Nos: 72 and 73
Distance from city centre: 19.8km/12ml
Walking distance: 27.4km/16.9ml
Amount of climbing: 465m/1525ft

An undulating walk through conifer forests and over high grazing land.

Park in Station Road, Eddleston. NT242471. To get there, drive S on the A701, through Penicuik, to Leadburn then take the A703 (continuation of same road) to Eddleston. Turn right on to Old Manse Road (signposted "Lyne via Meldons"), then left into Station Road.

Walk out of Eddleston along road towards Lyne to first cluster of buildings (Hattonknowe) and take second lane on right. At end continue ahead beside fence then turn left alongside a stone wall. After about 400yd go through gate on right and head NW (298°). Pass between house and broken barn then enter forest and climb a firebreak. At top of ridge cross wide cutting in the forest on to path which descends and swings round to right to reach forest road.

Go right for a few paces then left on another road, past some buildings (Greenside) to road end. Here continue straight ahead along a boggy firebreak for 1.4km/0.8ml. On emerging from forest go right. Cross Flemington

Saddle Yoke, Moffat Hills : walks 61 and 63

Burn, go through a gate, and climb a few yards to Green Knowe to farm track. Follow this left to next valley then go right on another track that traverses back E then N around Green Knowe. When the track flattens out cut up left to top of hill and follow ridge N to Wether Law (479m/1571ft. TP).

Head NE (44°) off the summit towards small tree-covered hill. On the saddle, climb over stone wall into forest and up firebreak directly ahead. At top of the hill turn right (E) down another firebreak then right along forestry road for 1km/0.6ml to widening of the road (turning area). Here go SE (120°), along a firebreak, over ridge of Cloich Hills then left along forestry road. At Cloich Farm go through gate on right and head SE across grazing land and moor to line of trees. Follow these S to junction of paths and start of stone wall beside the trees. Pass through gate in wall and follow path through woods past back of Black Barony Hotel until hotel service road is reached. Walk down this a few paces then take access road back to starting place.

To shorten the walk, at Greenside go right instead of left along forestry road to Cloich Farm then across fields as above to Black Barony Hotel and Eddleston. Save 10.5km/6.5ml.

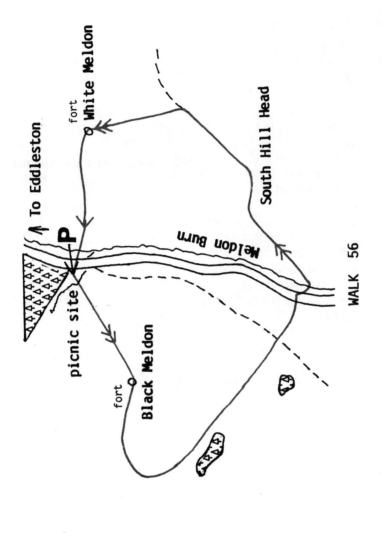

To Eddleston

White Meldon
fort

P

picnic site

Black Meldon
fort

Meldon Burn

South Hill Head

WALK 56

N

56. The Meldons

Ordnance Survey map No: 73
Distance from city centre: 25.2km/15.7ml
Walking distance: 7.5km/4.6ml
Amount of climbing: 453m/1485ft

A short easy walk over the two hills that guard the pass between Eddleston and Lyne. Superb views over the Tweed valley from the summits. There are several sites of archaeological interest in the area.

Park at the Meldons picnic site. NT212429. To get there drive on the A701, through Penicuik, to Leadburn then take the A703 (continuation of same road). At Eddleston, turn right into Old Manse Road (signposted "Lyne via Meldons") and drive on for another 6km/3.7ml to the end of the forest.

Climb up behind toilets, cross the burn and take one of the paths through the bracken directly ahead (245°) up to large cairn on top of Black Meldon (407m/1335ft). Just below the summit you will cross a line of rocks that were once the walls of an ancient fort.

Head W to second, slightly lower summit then descend ridge S (162°) to small conifer plantation and follow stone wall down to a farm track. Cross the track and follow the gully the short remaining distance to the road.

Cross the road, Meldon Burn and fence, then climb up to the right for 100m/330ft to join path that gradually ascends towards the NE (49°). Follow this, past a large stone-walled sheep enclosure, to saddle between White Meldon and South Hill Head. Here turn N and follow ridge up on to White Meldon (427m/1400ft. TP. Cairn, ancient fort).

Descend W, past the remains of a number of ancient settlements, to the picnic site.

To shorten the walk, omit either Black Meldon (save 1.2km/0.7ml); or White Meldon (save 1.5km/0.9ml).

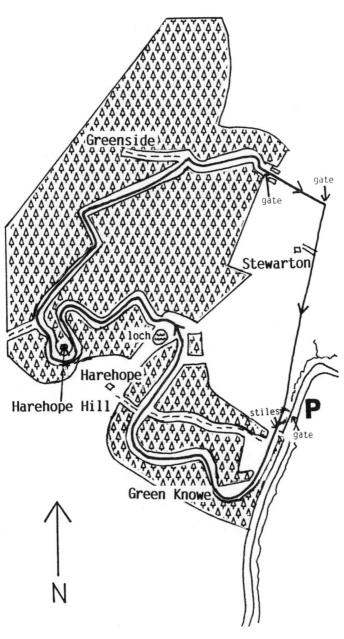

Greenside

gate

gate

Stewarton

loch

Harehope

Harehope Hill

Green Knowe

stiles

P

gate

N

WALK 57

57.   Harehope Hill

Ordnance Survey map Nos: 72 and 73
Distance from city centre: 24km/14ml
Walking distance: 17.4km/10.8ml
Amount of climbing: 177m/580ft

A pleasant, gentle walk through Cloich Hills Forest. Several interesting sites of antiquity en route.

Park at Nether Stewarton entrance to the forest. (Do not obstruct entrance.) NT217440. To get there, drive S on the A701 to Leadburn then the A703 (continuation of same road) to Eddleston. Turn right on to "Lyne via Meldons" road and drive on for another 4.5km/2.8ml.

Enter the forest and turn left (S) at fire post, on to track of old road. After crossing two stiles you will reach the access road to Harehope Farm. Cross this road and continue S along a forestry road. Note sites of ancient settlements close to bend in road.

Follow the road round to a T-junction. Here go right then left on to another forestry road. Follow this past a small loch, over open ground then back into the forest, round a large, circular ancient settlement, then up to the top of Harehope Hill (395m/1295ft) Remains of hill fort, with a splendid view across the valley of Lyne Water.

Stay on the road a little further until it swings round to W then go NE (38°) along a firebreak to another forestry road. Follow this left to top of ridge then turn ENE (62°) along a wider firebreak that follows the ridge.

After 1.4km/0.8ml, at small yellow markers, turn right (ESE, 106°) on to a footpath that descends to gate at the edge of the forest. Climb over gate, pass between house and old barn then follow farm track SE to gate in stone wall. Go through, turn right and follow wall to Stewarton Farm. Pass by farm buildings then, still on same track (old road), walk through forest back to starting point.

To shorten the walk, from Harehope Hill return along forestry road used on outward journey to a T-junction, turn left and keep going to asphalt road. Parking place is a few yards to left. Save 3.1km/1.9ml.

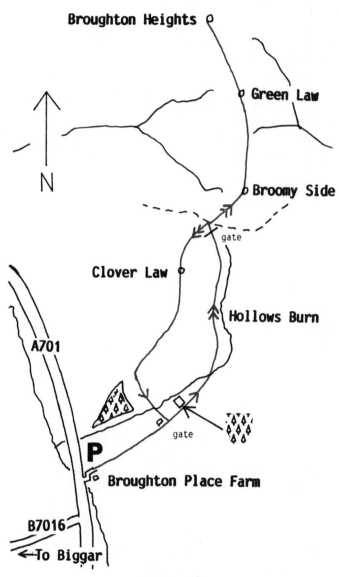

Broughton Heights

Green Law

Broomy Side

gate

Clover Law

Hollows Burn

A701

Broughton Place Farm

gate

P

B7016

To Biggar

N

WALK 58

58. *Broughton Heights*

Ordnance Survey map No: 72

Distance from city centre: 45km/28ml

Walking distance: 14.7km/9ml

Amount of climbing: 565m/1860ft

Excellent walking on rolling grassy tops. If the weather is fine, the views are marvellous.

Park car in avenue near Broughton Place Farm. NT113371. To get there, take the A702 to Biggar then the B7016 E to join the A701 at Broughton. Go N along the A701 for a few yards then right along farm access road, round farm buildings, to end of avenue.

Walk straight on, with castle-shaped building on right, along old drove road passing through gate near house on left, small woodland on left, then fording Hollows Burn. The track then becomes a path up the left side of glen to col between Clover Law and Broomy Side. Pass through gate and turn up Broomy Side (501m/1634ft), along to Green Law (547m/1794ft) and Broughton Heights (571m/1873ft. TP) – the best view in the Southern Uplands.

Return to col between Broomy Side and Clover Law. Ascend Clover Law (493m/1617ft). Go along ridge and drop down before woodland to Hollows Burn. Cross this, go on to road, and right to car.

It is not practicable to shorten this walk, except by turning back before reaching Broughton Heights.

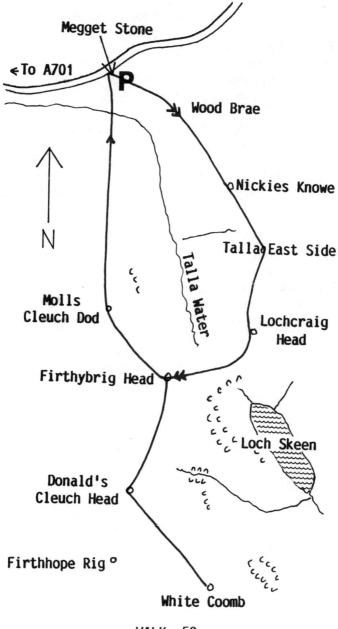

Megget Stone

←To A701

P

Wood Brae

Nickies Knowe

Talla East Side

Talla Water

Molls
Cleuch Dod

Lochcraig
Head

Firthybrig Head

Loch Skeen

Donald's
Cleuch Head

Firthhope Rig

White Coomb

N

WALK 59

MOFFAT HILLS

59. *White Coomb*

Ordnance Survey map Nos: 72 and 79
Distance from city centre: 66.6km/41.2ml
Walking distance: 20.4km/12.7ml
Amount of climbing: 572m/1876ft

An excellent walk over several hills above 2500ft including the highest of the Moffat Hills.

Park near the Megget Stone on the top of the Tweedsmuir – St Mary's Loch Pass. NT150203. To get there, take the A701 through Penicuik, fork right at Leadburn and continue along A701 to Tweedsmuir. Here turn left, past Talla Reservoir, and climb to top of pass.

Strike out on to the hills heading SE up Wood Brae, over Nickies Knowe, then up Talla Side East on to Lochcraig Head. Now follow the Regional Boundary fence SW down into a col then up on to Firthybrig Head (763m/2504ft). Go S beside a dyke over Donald's Cleuch Head to Firthhope Rig (801m/2627ft) then SE to White Coomb (821m/2659ft. Cairn); the highest of the Moffat Hills and a Corbett.

Return to Firthybrig Head then follow dyke NW over Molls Cleuch Dod and down ridge to start.

To shorten the walk, turn at Firthybrig Head (omitting Donald's Cleuch Head and White Coomb). Save 7.6km/4.7ml.

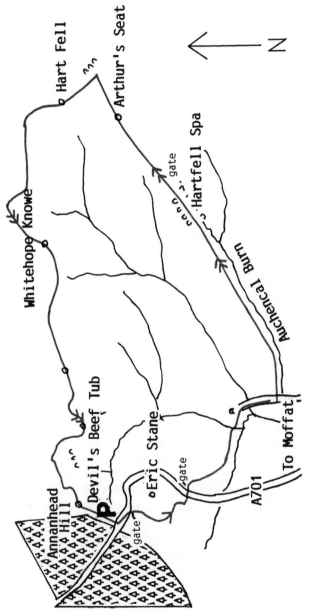

Hart Fell

Arthur's Seat

Whitehope Knowe

gate

Hartfell Spa

Auchencat Burn

N

WALK 60

Devil's Beef Tub

Eric Stane

gate

Annanhead Hill

P

gate

To Moffat

A701

60. Hart Fell and Devil's Beef Tub

Ordnance Survey map No: 78
Distance from city centre: 72km/45ml.
Walking distance: 25km/15.4ml
Amount of climbing: 860m/2820ft

A superb high-level walk to Hart Fell returning around the brim of the 300m/1000ft-deep Devil's Beef Tub.

Park in lay-by on A701 overlooking the Devil's Beef Tub. NT056127. To get there, drive S on the A701 almost to Moffat. The lay-by is on the left approximately 3km/2ml beyond signpost indicating the source of the River Tweed.

Walk down road to left-hand bend, go through gate on right and follow grass track round Eric Stane (site of Roman signal station) back to A701. Go through gate opposite and descend on farm track to a bridge over a burn. Just before the bridge, turn left and walk down to farm then along asphalt road to signpost on left for foot-path to Hartfell Spa.

Follow the marked way beside Auchencal Burn and up scree-sided gully to Hartfell Spa, a man-made cave over a natural spring. Continue up gully to top (some scrambling required) or climb loose scree on right. At top go through gate in fence and follow grass track then path on to Arthur's Seat. The path now skirts the top of a steep-sided valley with views across to Swatte Fell. At head of valley turn NW (312°) beside fence to TP (enclosed within a cairn) on Hart Fell (808m/2650ft – a Corbett).

Head NNW (340°) beside fence for 500yd then WNW (292°) down steep grassy slope to boggy col. Cross over and climb opposite bank on to Whitehope Knowe (614m/2013ft). Continue climbing on to Whitehope Heights then head W over a series of small hills around the Devil's Beef Tub (head of the Annan Valley) to Annanhead Hill (478m/1567ft. TP), then down beside fence and edge of woodland to lay-by on A701.

For a shorter walk start off by climbing Annanhead Hill, descend into col then descend narrow path into the Devil's Beef Tub and on to asphalt road. Save 5km/3ml.

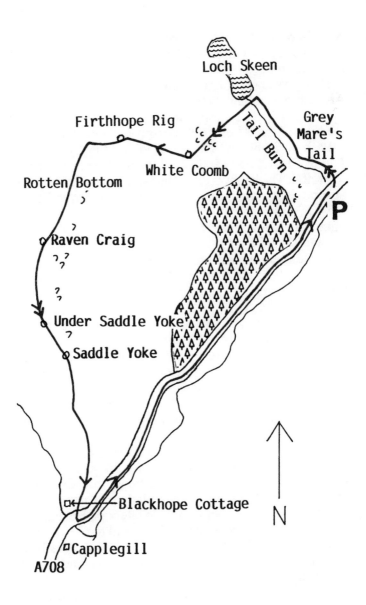

Loch Skeen

Firthhope Rig

Grey Mare's Tail

Tail Burn

White Coomb

Rotten Bottom

P

Raven Craig

Under Saddle Yoke

Saddle Yoke

N

Blackhope Cottage

Capplegill

A708

WALK 61

61. West Ridge of Moffat Dale

Ordnance Survey map Nos: 78 and 79
Distance from city centre: 97km/60ml
Walking distance: 22.7km/14ml
Amount of climbing: 767m/2515ft

This is a most satisfying route taking in the 60m/200ft Grey Mare's Tail waterfall, Loch Skeen, White Coomb (a Corbett) and a knife-edge ridge over Saddle Yoke.

Leave vehicle in Grey Mare Tail's carpark, Moffat Dale. NT186145. To get there, take the A701 through Penicuik to Moffat then the A708 (signposted "Selkirk") for 16km/10ml up the Moffat Valley.

Go up the established path to right of Tail Burn, past Grey Mare's Tail waterfall, up to Loch Skeen. Ford burn at loch then head SW across heather and wet grassland and up on to White Coomb (822m/2696ft), the highest of the Moffat Hills and a Corbett.

Walk along ridge WNW to Firthhope Rig (801m/2627ft) then follow new fence W then SW down to saddle between the Gameshope and Carrifran valleys. This is aptly named "Rotten Bottom"; it is wet and very boggy. Cross, keeping well left to avoid the worst areas, climb over small hill above Raven Craig (crags not visible from this point) then climb S on to Under Saddle Yoke (745m/2443ft). From here Ravens Craig and the impressive scree slopes of Black Hope Glen are clearly visible.

There now follows a most exhilarating ridge walk over Saddle Yoke (a subsidiary top of Under Saddle Yoke) and down to the road at Capplegill. This grassy ridge is extremely narrow with 450m/1500ft drops on either side. Not for the faint-hearted! From Capplegill walk along road to carpark (6.5km/4ml), or hitch a lift from a passing motorist.

To shorten the walk, descend E from White Coomb, over Rough Craigs to Upper Tarnberry then down beside forest (so as to avoid crags to left). Save 15.6km/9.5ml.

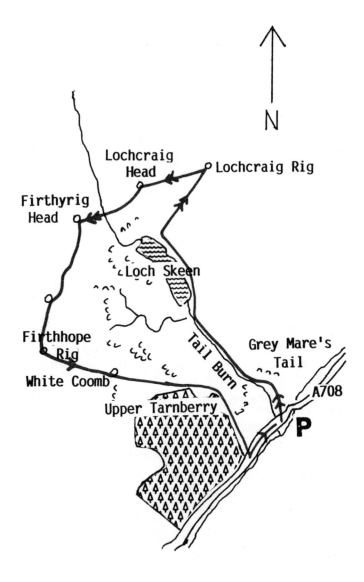

WALK 62

62.   Grey Mare's Tail and Loch Skeen
Ordnance Survey map No: 79
Distance from city centre: 97.4km/60.4ml
Walking distance: 18km/11.2ml
Amount of climbing: 695m/2279ft

An enjoyable circuit of a justifiably popular glen. From White Coomb it is possible to see the Eildon Hills and the Cheviots to the E and the Solway Firth and Helvellyn to the S.

Leave vehicle in Grey Mare's Tail carpark. NT186145. To get there, take the A701 through Penicuik to Moffat then the A708 (signposted "Selkirk") for 16km/10ml up the Moffat Valley.

Go up the established path to right of Tail Burn, past Grey Mare's Tail waterfall, to Loch Skeen. Follow path around E bank of loch then head NE, over wall, up on to Lochcraig Rig then SE up ridge on to Lochcraig Head. Follow wall and fence WSW over to Firthybrig Head then SSW along ridge to Firthhope Rig. Here leave the new fence and walk beside an old fence ESE to White Coomb (822m/2696ft), the highest of the Moffat Hills and a Corbett.

Descend E from White Coomb, over Rough Craigs to Upper Tarnberry then down beside forest (so as to avoid dangerous crags to left) to road.

To shorten the walk, ford Tail Burn at outlet of Loch Skeen then head SW across heather and wet grassland and up on to White Coomb. Save 8.1km/5ml.

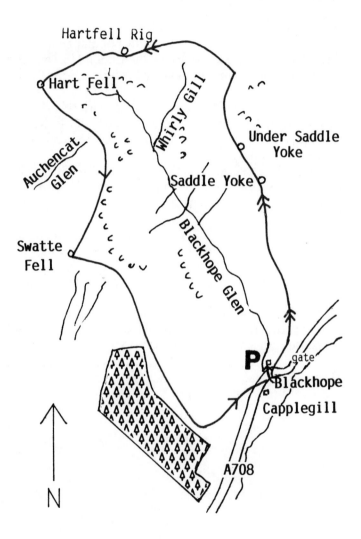

Hartfell Rig

Hart Fell

Whirly Gill

Under Saddle Yoke

Auchencat Glen

Saddle Yoke

Swatte Fell

Blackhope Glen

P

gate

Blackhope

Capplegill

A708

N

WALK 63

63.   Black Hope

Ordnance Survey map No: 78
Distance from city centre: 91km/56.4ml
Walking distance: 21km/11.2ml
Amount of climbing: 923m/3027ft

This walk encircles the beautiful Blackhope Glen. The outward route traverses a narrow ridge with views down into the glen and across the 450m/1500ft scree-covered southern face. The return is over Hart Fell, one of the highest Moffat Hills, and Swatte Fell.

Leave vehicle at Capplegill, just N of bridge over Blackhope Burn, near Blackhope Cottage. NT147098. To get there, take the A701 through Penicuik to Moffat then the A708 (signposted "Selkirk") for 9.6km/6ml up the Moffat Valley.

Go through the gate next to Blackhope Cottage on to a track that runs the length of the glen. After a few paces cut up right through bracken then climb grassy ridge up to and over Saddle Yoke (735m/2410ft) and Under Saddle Yoke (745m/2443ft). This ridge is very narrow and ex-posed, especially near the top where the steep, grassy slopes drop away for 450m/1500ft on either side. Head down to the N then circle round the head of Whirly Gill, climb W on to Hartfell Rig and follow fence up ridge on to Hart Fell (808m/2650ft. TP hidden among rocks) which is a Corbett.

Head SE, beside fence, around head of the deep Auchencat Glen and along edge of Blackhope Glen, to Swatte Fell (728m/2387ft). Descend SE shoulder, close to forest so as to avoid the crags of Hang Gill, towards road. Near the bottom there is a track that leads down to Capplegill Farm.

To shorten the walk, scramble down Whirly Gill and follow the track through the bottom of the glen back to Blackhope Cottage. Save 6.7km/4.1ml.

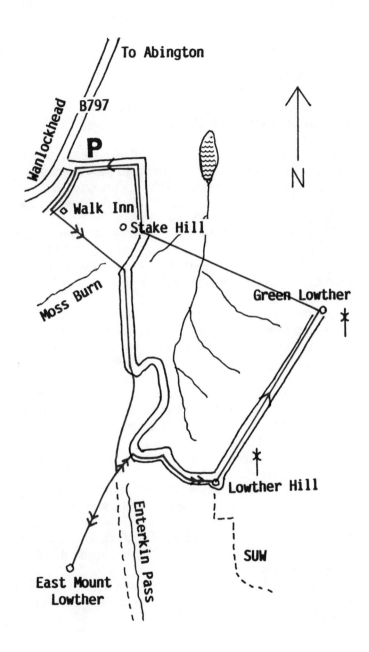

To Abington

B797

Wanlockhead

P

Walk Inn

Stake Hill

Moss Burn

Green Lowther

Lowther Hill

SUW

Enterkin Pass

East Mount Lowther

N

WALK 64

CENTRAL SOUTHERN UPLANDS

64.   Lowther Hill

Ordnance Survey map No: 71 or 78
Distance from city centre: 77km/47.7ml
Walking distance: 14.2km/8.8ml
Amount of climbing: 464m/1522ft

This mixture of road and rough path takes you to the "top of the world' – a Southern Uplands high-level walk.

Park at Wanlockhead (the highest village in Scotland) about 90m/100yd along road to Lowther Hill. NS880131. To get there, take A702 to Abington then B797 to Wanlockhead. The road to Lowther Hill is on the northern outskirts of village.

The area around Wanlockhead is rich in minerals, particularly gold and lead, and has been mined intermittently since Roman times, particularly during the 18th and 19th centuries. A railway was built to serve the mines at the beginning of the century but it was closed with most of the mines in 1938.

Walk back towards the village to point where the road is crossed by track of the old railway and follow the latter S to the Walk Inn. Here turn left and follow Southern Upland Way (marked by brown posts with yellow arrows and white insignia) past Stake Hill and Moss Burn to rejoin Lowther Hill road. Where road swings left, leave it and head SSW down to col then

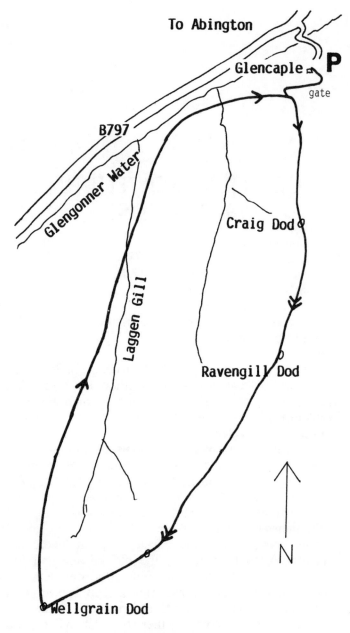

To Abington

Glencaple

P

gate

B797

Glengonner Water

Craig Dod

Laggen Gill

Ravengill Dod

N

Wellgrain Dod

WALK 65

up on to East Mount Lowther (631m/2069ft). To the left of the col is the Enterkin Pass, an old route between Dumfries and the North and site where soldiers escorting prisoners to Edinburgh were ambushed by local Covenanters.

Return to col then go uphill, rejoin road and follow it to radar station on the summit of Lowther Hill (725m/ 2378ft) then NW to Green Lowther (732m/2403ft. TP. Radio mast). Descend WNW, cross burn then climb Stake Hill as far as the Lowther road. Follow the road to the right back to the starting point.

To shorten the walk, omit East Mount Lowther. Save 4.2km/2.6ml.

65. Wellgrain Dod
Ordnance Survey map No: 71
Distance from city centre: 67.5km/42ml
Walking distance: 12.7km/7.9ml
Amount of climbing: 308m/1010ft

A gentle walk in sheep-rearing country.

Park at Glencaple, a shepherd's cottage, near Abington. NS920214. To get there, take the A702 through Biggar to Abington then the B797. After 1.2km/0.8ml turn left and follow road across Glengonnar Water to Glencaple.

Walk past the shepherd's cottage then turn right along track beside wall. At gate turn left and follow wall round to left then climb ridge to Craig Dod (436m/1439ft) and on to Ravengill Dod (538m/1765ft. TP). Continue along ridge, heading SW, over two more hills then up on to Wellgrain Dod (553m/1814ft). Note that there are a number of shafts and entrances to old mine workings in the vicinity.

Return by heading N down ridge to the W of Laggen Gill to Glengonnar Water, then along farm track to Glencaple.

It is not practicable to shorten this walk.

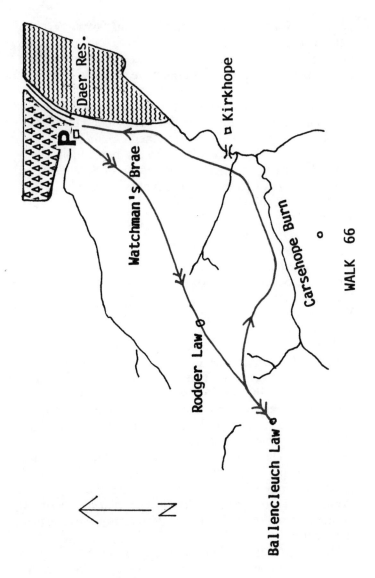

Daer Res.

Kirkhope

Watchman's Brae

Rodger Law ∘

Carsehope Burn

Ballencleuch Law ∘

WALK 66

N ←

66.   *Ballencleuch Law and Rodger Law*

Ordnance Survey map No: 78
Distance from city centre: 85km/53ml
Walking distance: 13.6km/8.4ml
Amount of climbing: 379m/1243ft

A high-level walk after a steep climb overlooking Daer Reservoir.

Park car at end of forestry on W side of Daer Reservoir. NS966076. To get there, go via A702 (Biggar Road) to Abington then S along A74. After 7.4km/4.5ml turn right on to A702 then, after 5.8km/3.6ml, left along minor road to Daer Reservoir.

Head SW (220°) up steep slopes to Watchman's Brae (596m/1954ft) then WSW (246°) to Rodger Law (688m/2256ft. TP). From here go SW (228°) to Ballencleuch Law (691m/2266ft).

Return by retracing your steps to col, then go down to Carsehope Burn and follow it to Kirkhope. Walk along road (1.6km/1ml) to start.

To shorten the walk, return from Rodger Law by outward route. Save 6km/3.7ml.

Black Hope Glen : walks 61 and 63

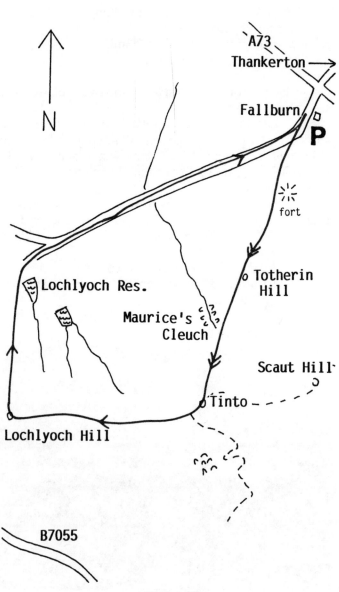

N

A73
Thankerton →

Fallburn

P

fort

Lochlyoch Res.

o Totherin
Hill

Maurice's
Cleuch

Scaut Hill

o Tinto

Lochlyoch Hill

B7055

WALK 67

67. Tinto

Ordnance Survey map No: 72
Distance from city centre: 54.3km/33.8ml
Walking Distance: 16.5km/10.2ml
Amount of climbing: 562m/1725ft

A prominent landmark in the Clyde Valley which is easy to climb.

Park in minor road off A73 at Fallburn (near Thankerton). NS965376. To get there, take A702 to Biggar, then A72 W, and finally A73 NW. The minor road is on the left 2.1km/1.3ml beyond the A72/A73 junction.

Leave carpark and continue along minor road for short distance, then follow clearly marked path on left uphill. Shortly you will see on the left the well-preserved remains of a fort (c.1000BC). The route becomes steeper, then passes Totherin Hill (479m/1571ft), and Maurice's Cleuch corrie, to the summit of Tinto (707m/2335ft. TP), also called Tintock Tap. It is said there was a Druid temple here. The extremely large cairn is from the bronze age (c.1000-3000BC), but the story goes that the local people carried the stones to the top as a penance.

Return by walking W along ridge to Lochlyock Hill (529m/1735ft), then N downhill to Lochlyock Reservoir and NE along road to Fallburn.

To shorten the walk, return from Tinto by outward route. Save 6km/3.7ml.

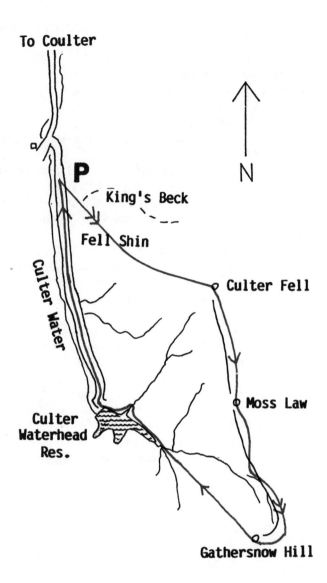

To Coulter

P

King's Beck

Fell Shin

Culter Water

Culter Fell

Culter
Waterhead
Res.

Moss Law

N

Gathersnow Hill

WALK   68

68. Culter Fell and Gathersnow Hill

Ordnance Survey map No: 72
Distance from city centre: 54km/33.2ml
Walking distance: 18.5km/11.5ml
Amount of climbing: 718m/2355ft

Quite a long hard walk, but very enjoyable.

Park car in Culter Water road at foot of King's Beck. NT032307. To get there, go via Biggar Road (A702), through Biggar. When main road turns right at Coulter, go straight on along side road and follow sign "Birthwood". After 2.9km/1.8ml take left fork. Then pass Birthwood entrance by keeping to road which turns left then right. Soon you are at King's Beck. There is a small, roofless, stone building on right of road and a place to park on left.

Climb steeply SE (140°) over Fell Shin to Culter Fell (748m/2455ft. TP. Cairn). This is on the Strathclyde/Borders Regional Boundary. Following line of fence, descend SSE (165°) by Moss Law to Holm Nick, then climb Gathersnow Hill (690m/2263ft). Descend NW (316°) to Culter Waterhead Reservoir and go round NE (right) side. Complete the walk by Culter Water to car.

To shorten the walk, from Culter Fell go down by Lang Gill to Culter Waterhead (omitting Moss Law and Gathersnow Hill). Save 6.4km/4ml.

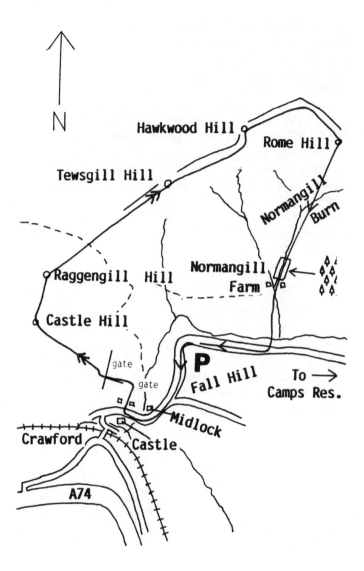

WALK 69

69.   Crawford Hills

Ordnance Survey map No: 72
Distance from city centre: 72.3km/45ml
Walking distance: 16km/10ml
Amount of climbing: 536m/1758ft

A typical and delightful Southern Uplands hill walk. Not difficult but best avoided in mist. This was a gold mining area in the 1500s and Crawford gold was used in the crowns of the Scottish kings.

Park car at side of Camps Reservoir road near Fall Hill. NS963222. To get there take the A702 then the A74 to Crawford. Turn left at signpost "Camps", pass over railway and turn left again. Go over River Clyde, turn right and pass the ruins of Crawford Castle and Midlock. At next junction go left (away from Midlock Water). On right is Fall Hill (site of ancient crematorium c.2000BC).

Walk back along road to Crawford Castle (captured from the English by William Wallace in the 13th century, later used by King James V as a hunting-box). Turn right along road between house and farm, through a gate, and along old road to another gate. Go through this gate, turn left and follow dyke to fence. Go over another gate a little along to the right and climb Castle Hill (483m/1586ft).

Head NNE (25°) across to Raggengill Hill (474m/1556ft). Descend into bealach (through which the Abington-Normangill path passes) then climb, beside dyke, to top of Tewsgill Hill (569m/1867ft. TP). Continue beside dyke to Hawkwood Hill then turn right and climb Rome Hill (565m/1852ft).

Descend to SW then follow Normangill Burn through a small woodland and past Normangill Farm to asphalt road. The mounds to the left, on either side of the road, are the remains of a circular henge (prehistoric place of ritual). Turn right and walk along road to car.

To shorten the walk, head SE from Tewsgill Hill to Normangill Farm (omitting Hawkwood Hill and Rome Hill). Save 3.9km/2.4ml.

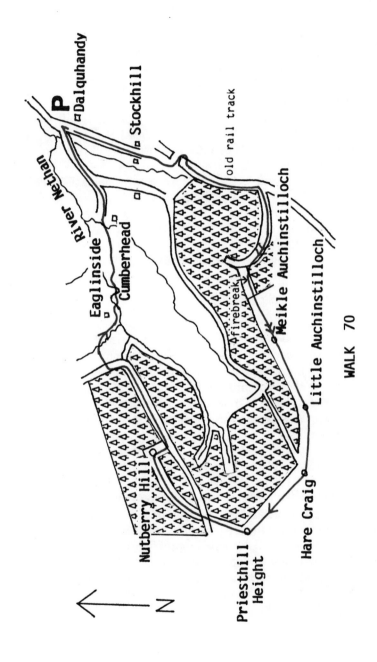

WALK 70

70. Auchinstilloch and Nutberry Hills

Ordnance Survey map No: 71

Distance from city centre: 68.4km/42.4ml

Walking distance: 22.4km/14ml

Amount of climbing: 376m/1233ft

An easy walk through forest, grass and moorland.

Park at Dalquhandy near Lesmahagow. NS788351. To get there, take the A70 and A743 to Lanark, the A72 W for 3km/2ml then the B7018 to Lesmahagow. Cross the A74 (left then right) and follow road through Lesmahagow towards Coalburn. At golf course, turn right, pass club-house, then next left. Go straight ahead at crossroads then left on to farm road (marked "Stockhill") and park.

Walk along road past Dalquhandy farm to Stockhill Farm. Pass straight through, between barn and outhouses, on to farm track across fields to gap in old railway embankment. Go through gate on right and follow railway track into forest. After 1.6km/1ml turn right on to forestry road as far as a sharp bend to the right. Here go left through a firebreak to the forest boundary then SW, across heather moorland, parallel with edge of forest, to the summit of Meikle Auchinstilloch (491m/1609ft).

Continue alongside forest boundary fence, over Little Auchinstillloch to the flat, featureless top of Hare Craig, then head NW, past head of Ponesk Burn (source of the River Ayr), to Priesthill Height (492m/1615ft). Descend N, cross forestry road, then climb ridge between arms of forest on to Nutberry Hill (522m/1712ft. TP).

Descend SSE and go through firebreak to forest road. Turn left and follow road until it turns left and starts to climb. From here cut through trees on right, down to a small, deep valley. Follow this down to the remains of Eaglinside Farm then walk along a pleasant, grassy track, crossing the River Nethan several times, to Cumberhead then along the road back to Dalquhandy.

To shorten the walk, after Hare Craig, go NE down through trees to forestry road and follow it to the right back to the start. Save 2.9km/1.8ml.

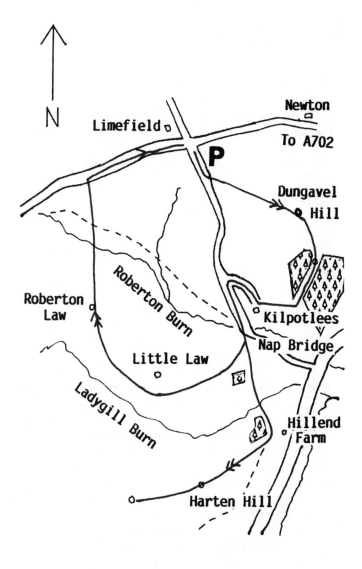

WALK 71

71. *Dungavel Hill and Roberton Law*

Ordnance Survey map No: 72

Distance from city centre: 61.7km/38.2ml

Walking distance: 27.6km/17ml

Amount of climbing: 483m/1584ft

This is an enjoyable walk over a prominent, cone-shaped hill and adjacent hills, which can be shortened to suit one's taste.

Park near Limefield crossroads. NS928314. To get there, take the A702 through Biggar and Coulter to the village of Lamington. Just beyond village turn right on to the B7055. Where the road turns sharp right at March-lands, go straight ahead on minor road, past Newton, to crossroads.

Walk S along road then leave on left side and climb to summit of Dungavel Hill (510m/1673ft. TP). Now head S to second summit. This is forested but there is a road through the trees to the top of the hill. Continue along forestry road until open ground is reached on the right then follow fence and wall W to Kilpotlees.

Go along the farm track down to an asphalt road and follow it S to Nap Bridge over Roberton Burn. Just over bridge turn right on farm track then cut across to small clump of trees on left. Pass to N of these and join track over Ladygill Burn and alongside woods near Hillend Farm. At end of woods climb on to ridge and follow it over both summits of Harten Hill (376m/1233ft. TP).

Retrace steps as far as track from Nap Bridge and follow track W around Little Law then head N to top of Roberton Law (377m/1237ft). Descend to the N, cross Roberton Burn once more then walk over to road. Turn right and return to starting point.

To shorten the walk, return along the road from Kilpotlees. Save 18.6km/11.5ml.

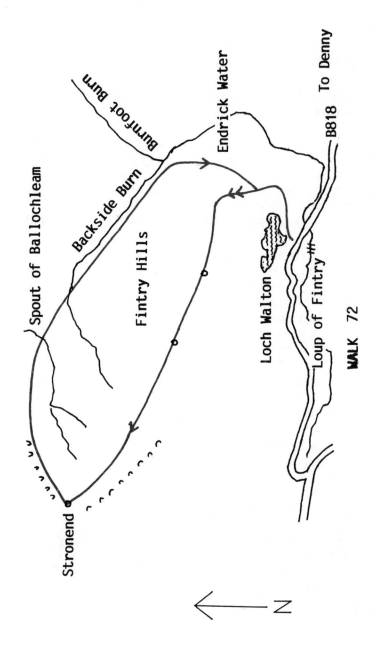

Burnfoot Burn

Endrick Water

Spout of Ballochleam

Backside Burn

Fintry Hills

Stronend

Loch Walton

B818   To Denny

Loup of Fintry

WALK 72

N

CAMPSIE FELLS AND FINTRY HILLS

72. *Fintry Hills*

Ordnance Survey map No: 57
Distance from city centre: 69km/42.8ml
Walking distance: 20.3km/12.6ml
Amount of climbing: 358m/1174ft

A good high-level walk on the Fintry Hills. An additional attraction is the Loup of Fintry, a spectacular waterfall, especially following rain, on the River Endrick close to the parking place.

Park on the edge of the B818 (Denny to Fintry road) close to the entrance to Loch Walton. NS664864. To get there, take the M9 to jct. 8, the M876 to jct. 1, then the A883 to Denny. Leave via the B818 (signposted "Fintry") and follow it until 1.3km/0.8ml beyond Carron Valley Reservoir.

Walk around the E end of Loch Walton, climb N on to ridge, then head NW over the flat tops of the Fintry Hills to Stronend (512m/1679ft. TP disguised by pieces of natural stone fixed to its side. Cairn). Now head NE then SE along edge of escarpment and top of line of crags to Spout of Ballochleam. Return by heading SE beside Backside Burn as far as the point where it is joined by Burnfoot Burn then cut across S to Loch Walton and thence back to starting point.

To shorten the walk, retrace route from Stronend back to start. Save 3km/1.9ml.

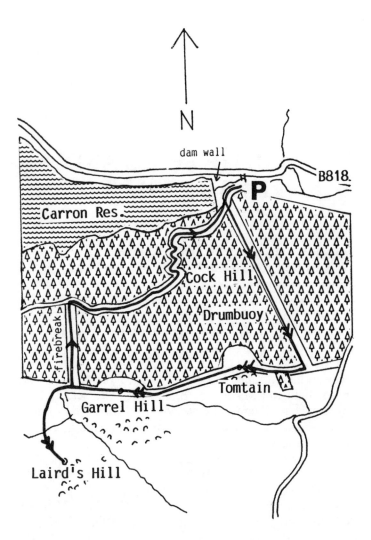

N

dam wall

B818.

Carron Res.

P

Cock Hill

Drumbuoy

firebreak

Tomtain

Garrel Hill

Laird's Hill

WALK 73

73. Kilsyth Hills

Ordnance Survey map No: 64
Distance from city centre: 62km/38.3ml
Walking distance: 21km/13ml
Amount of climbing: 387m/1269ft

A pleasant ramble over the Kilsyth Hills and through Carron Valley Forest on paths and forestry tracks.

Leave vehicle in forestry carpark/picnic site, Carron Valley. NS721838. To get there, take the M9 to jct. 8, the M876 to jct. 1, then the A883 to crossroads in centre of Denny. Go straight across, through Duke Street, to T-junction. Here go left and immediately right on to B818 (signposted "Fintry"). The entrance to the picnic site is on the left, 2km/1.2ml beyond the Carronbridge Hotel.

Start along marked forest walks behind toilets. Ignore the red, yellow and blue arrows and keep going straight ahead, beside dyke, through forest ride over the eastern shoulders of Cock Hill and Drumbuoy. This path is infrequently used and a little overgrown with grass and rushes. On emerging from forest, turn right and follow grass track up on to Tomtain (453m/1484ft. TP).

Descend W to edge of forest. In the wall just here there is a stone from a demolished building bearing the inscription "Built in 1856 by A. Dennistoun". Continue along edge of forest, over Garrel Hill (458m/1503ft), and down to dyke. Turn left, beside dyke, cross a burn, and climb on to Laird's Hill (425m/1393ft).

Return to position at forest reached on outward journey, after descent from Garrel Hill, and before turning off to Laird's Hill. Look for firebreak. Follow this N. After a little it descends steeply then meets a forestry road. Turn right along this. At first junction turn left (down), and later (nearer the reservoir) turn right. This takes you back to carpark.

For a much shorter walk, start from the Tak-ma-Doon Road (left at Carronbridge Hotel) at the SE corner of the forest (NS735814) and walk along the

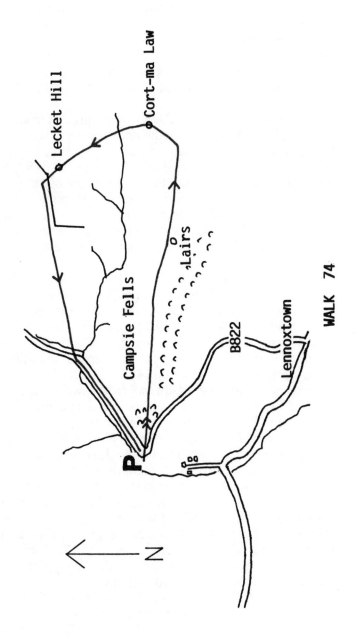

Lecket Hill

Cort-ma Law

Lairs

Campsie Fells

B822

Lennoxtown

P

N

WALK 74

grass track over Tomtain and Garrel Hill to Laird's Hill. Return by same route. Distance is 15.6km/ 9.6ml.

74.   Cort-ma Law and Lecket Hill

Ordnance Survey map No: 64

Distance from city centre: 75.6km/46.6ml

Walking distance: 13.5km/8.4ml

Amount of climbing: 326m/1069ft

A typical Campsie Fell plateau walk. Can be very boggy in wet weather.

Leave vehicle in carpark above Campsie Glen. NS613801. To get there, take the M9 to jct. 8, the M876 to jct. 5 then the M80 to jct. 4. From there follow the A803 via Kilsyth then the A891. Turn right at Lennoxtown on to the B822 (Crow Road). The carpark is on the left, at the bend, 3.2km/2ml from Lennoxtown.

Cross road and follow path heading E on to then along top of Campsie Fells escarpment to Lairs (504m/ 1652ft. Cairns) continue E, past cairns, to the flat-topped Cort-ma Law (531m/1742ft. TP).

Head N then NW over moorland to Lecket Hill (546m/1792ft. Cairn). Head N a few paces to fence, climb over, turn left and look for old boundary stone. Then follow fence WSW (258°) until it turns left and descends into valley. Continue on path down ridge to road then walk along road back to carpark. Note Jamie Wright's Well to left of road shortly before carpark.

It is impractical to shorten this walk other than turning back at Cort-ma Law.

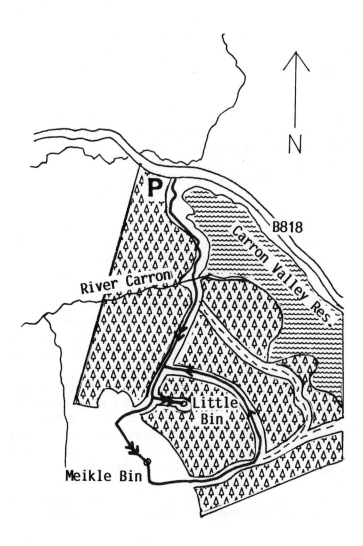

P

B818

Carron Valley Res.

River Carron

Little
Bin

Meikle Bin

WALK 75

75. *Little Bin and Meikle Bin*

Ordnance Survey map Nos: 57 and 64
Distance from city centre: 68km/42ml
Walking distance: 18km/11.2ml
Amount of climbing: 491m/1610ft

Quite a long walk but mostly on forest roads. Excellent views from summit.

Park at forest entrance on B818 at western end of Carron Valley Reservoir. NS672858. This reservoir was built in 1939 and considerably enlarged the existing loch. To get there, take the M9 to jct. 8, the M876 to jct. 1, then the A883 to crossroads in centre of Denny. Go straight across, through Duke Street, to T-junction. Here go left and immediately right on to B818 (signposted "Fintry") and follow it to the reservoir.

Walk S along forestry road, past two roads on the right, and cross bridge over river (Carron). At next junction go right. Further on pass a road on right. Shortly thereafter take right-hand fork and start climb on to NW shoulder of Little Bin. Where the road levels out and swings to left leave it and climb a firebreak on the left to the top of Little Bin (441m/1446ft).

Return to forestry road and continue walking along it until it reaches the NW ridge of Meikle Bin. Leave the road here and climb path up ridge to summit (570m/ 1870 ft. TP). Leave along the SE ridge, descending through forest until forestry road is encountered. Follow this NE to a junction on the edge of a clearing. Turn left and follow this road round the N of Little Bin to the junction with the road used on the outward journey, then follow outward route in reverse back to start.

To shorten the walk, omit Little Bin and return from Meikle Bin along outward route. Save 6.1km/3.8ml.

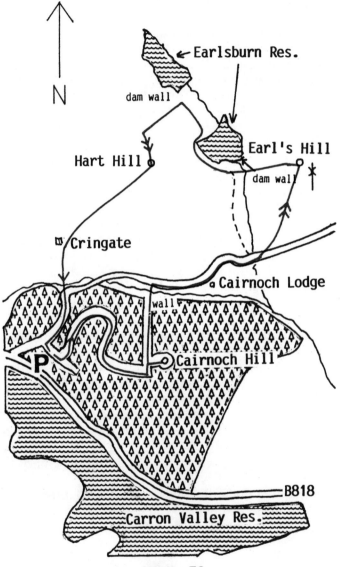

WALK 76

76.   Cairnoch Hill, Earl's Hill and Hart Hill

Ordnance Survey map No: 57

Distance from city centre: 68km/42ml

Walking distance: 20.3km/12.6ml

Amount of climbing: 402m/1318ft

A varied mixture of forestry road and moorland walking.

Park at remains of Dundaff Castle near Carron Valley Reservoir. NS682858. To get there, take the M9 to jct. 8, the M876 to jct. 1, then the A883 to Denny. Leave via the B818 (signposted "Fintry") and follow it to the western end of Carron Valley Reservoir. Turn right along road marked "Except for Access", then, in 500yd turn right on to a forestry road and park near open grassland with seats overlooking remains of castle.

Walk SE along forestry road, left at fork, then next right to eventually emerge from forest. Where road ends at a dyke, take path to left, beside wall, over brow of hill, then go right through a gap in wall and climb on to the summit of Cairnoch Hill (413m/1355ft. TP).

Return to stone wall and follow it N to a T-junction with another wall. Climb wall and accompanying fence (barbed and tricky) and cross over to road. Proceed to the right along road, past a side road to the left and across a bridge then cut NE over moorland to the radio masts on Earl's Hill (440m/1443ft).

Descend W to the lower of the two Earlsburn Reservoirs, cross the dam wall and follow the road up to the second reservoir. Now climb SW over moorland to a bealach then S to summit of Hart Hill (436m/1430ft). Descend SW, well into valley, then follow tractor tracks to ruins of Cringate Farm. Proceed S along access road then right at junction along asphalt road to forestry road and starting point.

To shorten the walk, on descending from Cairnoch Hill return left along road to start. Save 11.3km/7ml.

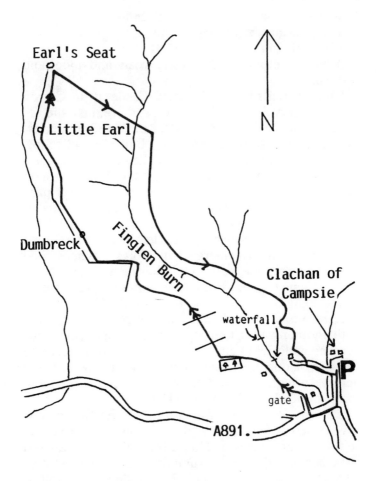

Earl's Seat

Little Earl

Dumbreck

Finglen Burn

Clachan of
Campsie

waterfall

gate

A891.

N

P

WALK 77

77.   *Earl's Seat*
Ordnance Survey map No: 64
Distance from city centre: 75km/46.2ml
Walking distance: 20km/12.4ml
Amount of climbing: 550m/1804ft

A most interesting and varied walk, though quite long. Not to be undertaken in misty weather.

Park car at Clachan of Campsie. NS610796. To get there, take the M9 to jct. 8, the M876 to jct. 5 then the M80 to jct. 4. From there follow the A803 via Kilsyth then the A891 past Lennoxtown turning off along road marked "Clachan of Campsie".

Walk back to A891, turn right, after 0.5km/0.3ml turn right along road marked "Morris of Glasgow". After passing the factory, proceed along farm road, through right gate, over rising field, to right side of ruined farm buildings. Then follow track towards right end of trees on hill, keeping Finglen Burn in sight on right. Note the waterfalls, called the Black Spout and, higher, the White Spout. When past woodlands, make for ridge of the hill, through gap in first dyke, then climb over second dyke. Keep up to wire fence and follow it (it has two opposite right hand turns) up to Dumbreck (508m/1665ft. TP). Then go N, still following fence, which is on the Strathclyde/Central Regional Boundary, avoiding some peat bog on the way by diverging slightly left, and so to Earl's Seat (578m/1896ft. TP), the highest hill in the Campsies.

Return by walking SE to cross Finglen Burn. Follow the burn, keeping just below the top of the hill. Use sheep paths where evident. After a deep gully, an old road track starts at a gate. This leads along hillside to Knowehead farm. Avoid going through the farm by cutting across and down field to gate in dyke. Go through gate and sharply down to road from farm. This leads down to Clachan of Campsie.

To shorten the walk, return from Dumbreck by outward route. Save 6km/3.7ml.

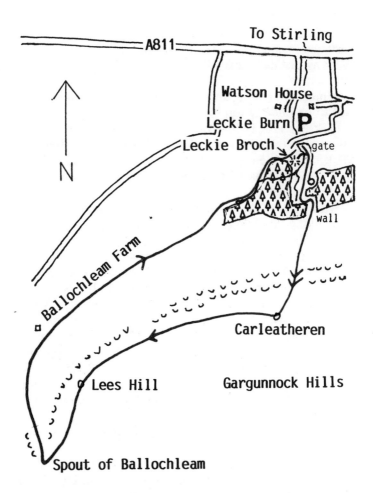

To Stirling

A811

Watson House

Leckie Burn **P**

Leckie Broch

gate

wall

Ballochleam Farm

Carleatheren

Gargunnock Hills

Lees Hill

Spout of Ballochleam

N

WALK 78

78.   Gargunnock Hills

Ordnance Survey map No: 57
Distance from city centre: 67.2km/41.5ml
Walking distance: 20.4km/12.7ml
Amount of climbing: 439m/1440ft

Quite a long walk but full of interesting features.

Park on side of access road to Watson House, NS699947, or in private road from that point, near Leckie Burn, NS691942. To get there, take the M9 to jct. 10, turn toward Stirling on the A84 and take the next road right through suburbs of Stirling. At T-junction with A811 go right then, after 9.6km/6ml, turn left on to minor road. At left-hand bend turn right into entrance to Watson House.

Go through small gate on S side of road near Leckie Burn and follow path on left of burn. After a short distance take path to right, cross burn and climb up to a large mound, the 2000-year-old Leckie Broch. Note the cup and ring markings on some of the rocks.

Retrace steps back across burn to main path and continue uphill. Watch out for an interesting old reservoir on the left (well worth the short detour). Where the path joins a forestry road go left then, after 100yd cut through trees on right to an old stone dyke. Climb over then head S up the escarpment on to Carleatheren (485m/1591ft. TP. Cairn).

Walk W along the edge of the escarpment, over Lees Hill, to Spout of Ballochleam. Now take the road down the escarpment towards Ballochleam Farm but leave it just before the farm and cut overland, beneath the escarpment, to meet the road at Leckie Burn.

To shorten the walk, return from Carleathern via outward route. Save 14.5km/9ml.

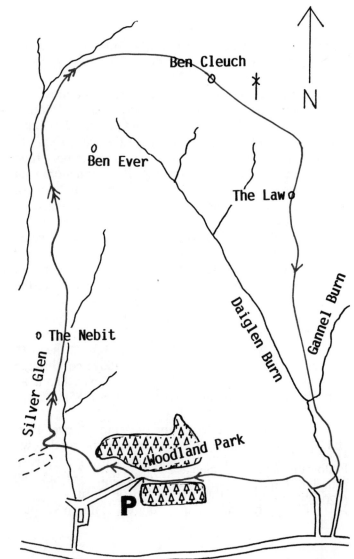

Ben Cleuch

Ben Ever

The Law

Gannel Burn

The Nebit

Daiglen Burn

Silver Glen

Woodland Park

P

Alva

Tillicoultry

N

WALK 79

OCHIL HILLS

79. Ben Cleuch
Ordnance Survey map No: 58
Distance from city centre: 60.7km/37.6ml
Walking distance: 15.6km/9.6ml
Amount of climbing: 669m/2194ft

Not difficult but quite a long climb, with interesting start and finish.

Leave car at picnic site and carpark in Woodland Park, Alva. NS898975. To get there, take the M9 to jct. 7 then M876/A876 over Kincardine Bridge. Turn left along A977, then left on A907 to Alloa and right along A908 towards Tillicoultry. At Fishcross turn left then right along to A91. Cross this road and go up minor road to Woodland Park.

Walk N then W along track, past golf course then Alva House stables, to join the Silver Glen footpath N of Alva. Follow the path up the glen and at its head swing right and round to Ben Cleuch ridge, and so along fence to summit (720m/2363ft. TP. Indicator). Sometimes the hill is called Glenwhappen Rig. There are two cairns on top.

Return by continuing along ridge past radio mast and via The Law (638m/2094ft) down to junction of Gannel Burn and Daiglen Burn. Cross the former and follow the path down to start of Tillicoultry. Cut across to W and follow track beside golf course to start.

It is not practicable to shorten this walk.

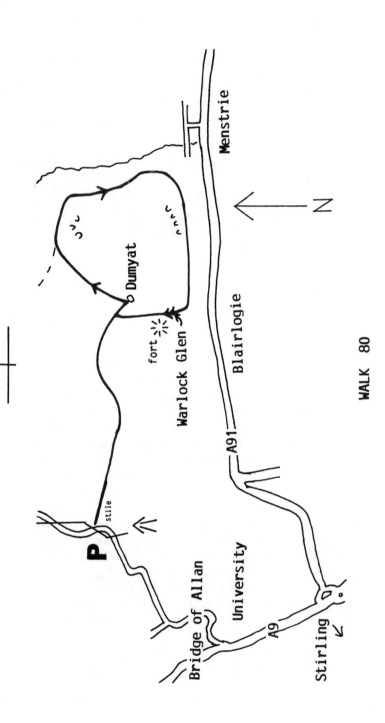

Menstrie

N

Dumyat

Blairlogie

fort

Warlock Glen

A91

WALK 80

P

stile

Bridge of Allan

University

A9

Stirling

80.   Dumyat
Ordnance Survey map Nos: 57 and 58
Distance from city centre: 66.5km/41.2ml
Walking distance: 11.2km/6.9ml
Amount of climbing: 540m/1771ft

An easy walk to a prominent top with outstanding views.

Park car in lay-by on minor road from Bridge of Allan to Sheriff Muir. NS813980. To get there, take M9 to jct. 10, then SE along A84 towards Stirling, but turning left over river (A9) to Causewayhead and then left (N) towards Bridge of Allan. Immediately past entrance to Stirling University, turn right to minor road (to Sheriffmuir). At fork go right. Parking is near overhead cables.

Go over stile on E side of road and follow path. Take the right fork near the start. Later the path turns uphill to the left and then to the right. Soon the summit of Dumyat (418m/1371ft. TP) is reached.

Return by descending path over SE shoulder steeply down towards Menstrie, but before reaching the road swinging W below Dumyat to join path from Blairlogie. This climbs up to Warlock Glen and a gorge. (Rock climbers come here. A 2000-year-old fort is on shoulder on the left). Go through glen and gorge and up to earlier route near summit. Turn left (W) and so back to start.

To shorten the walk, return directly from summit. Save 3.6km/2.2ml.

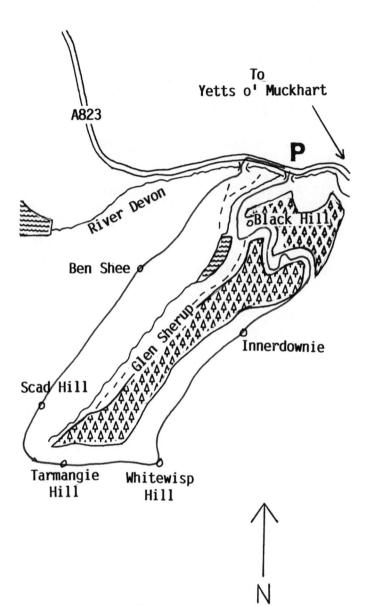

To
Yetts o' Muckhart

A823

P

River Devon

Black Hill

Ben Shee

Glen Sherup

Innerdownie

Scad Hill

Tarmangie
Hill

Whitewisp
Hill

N

WALK 81

81. *Round Glen Sherup*

Ordnance Survey map No: 58
Distance from city centre: 59.3km/36.3ml
Walking distance:21.3km/13.2ml
Amount of climbing: 590m/1935ft.

A long fine walk over broad smooth summits.

Park car at side of A823 (Glendevon) about 2km/1.3ml past Glendevon Inn. NN973053. To get there, cross Forth Bridge and take M90 to jct. 6. Then go W by A977, B918, A91 to Yetts o' Muckhart, and along A823.

Cross River Devon by bridge to old road through Whitens. Follow this round Black Hill and at junction go left (NE), which winds up to ridge. Continue climbing ridge (SW) to Innerdownie (611m/2004ft) and on to Whitewisp Hill (643m/2109ft). Then go W (271°) to Tarmangie Hill (645m/2115ft). Next go down (280°) to bealach at top of Glen Sherup and round (N) to Scad Hill (586m/1922ft). Follow down ridge (36°) and up to Ben Shee (515m/1689ft). Descend NE (50°) to River Devon and back to car.

To shorten the walk, descend where possible to forestry road in glen and return NE to start.

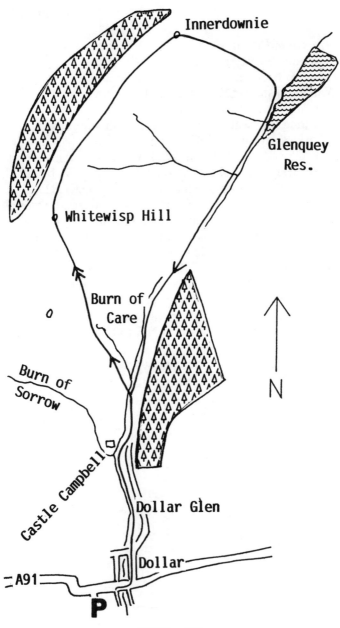

Innerdownie

Glenquey
Res.

Whitewisp Hill

Burn of
Care

Burn of
Sorrow

Castle Campbell

Dollar Glen

Dollar

A91

P

N

WALK 82

82.   Whitewisp Hill and Innerdownie
Ordnance Survey map No: 58
Distance from city centre: 54.3km/33.7ml
Walking distance: 18km/11ml
Amount of climbing: 644m/2112ft

A walk up the famous Dollar Glen, with an easier Ochil Hills walk.

Park car in Dollar on W side of river, at S side of A91. NS963979. To get there, cross the Forth Bridge and take the M90 to jct. 4. Head E on the B914 then B913 to Dollar.

Walk along the signposted footpath up Dollar Glen to Castle Campbell then follow the path N beside Burn of Care (not Burn of Sorrow to W of castle) until it divides into two streams. Cross the burn just before the division and climb up to the summit of Whitewisp Hill (643m/2110ft).

Strike NNE by dyke to Innerdownie (611m/2004ft). Return by dropping down to Glenquet Reservoir then following path SW back to Castle Campbell and on to Dollar.

To shorten the walk, return from Whitewisp Hill by outward route. Save 6.1km/3.8ml.

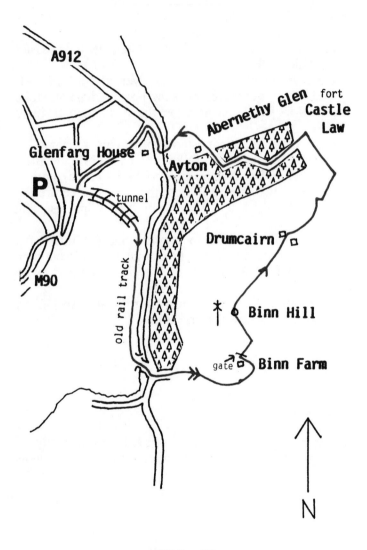

A912

Abernethy Glen   fort
                        Castle
                          Law

Glenfarg House

Ayton

P   tunnel

Drumcairn

M90

old rail track

Binn Hill

gate   Binn Farm

N

WALK 83

83. *Glen Farg and Binn Hill*

Ordnance Survey map No: 58
Distance from city centre: 64.8km/40.2ml
Walking distance: 15km/9.3ml
Amount of climbing: 285m/934ft

An undulating walk over agricultural and forest land. Part of route goes underground so a torch is essential.

Park at side of road close to dismantled railway bridge S of Bridge of Earn. NO153149. To get there, cross the Forth Road Bridge and take the M90 to jct. 9 then the A912 NW. At Bridge of Earn take the first road to the left (unclassified) to head SE and pass beneath the motorway. The old railway bridge is 2.7km/1.7ml farther along, close to the motorway.

Head E along the old railway track, through a long tunnel, and on up the glen to bridge just before a second tunnel. Scramble up left-hand embankment to top of bridge and follow farm track down to main road. Take minor road opposite up to Binn Farm (signposted). Here go through gate on right on to track heading NE then cut up to radio mast on Binn Hill (277m/908ft. TP).

Head NNE (30°) along ridge to some farm buildings (Drumcairn) then follow edge of a field NE until it meets the rocky slopes of Castle Law. Here, step over fence and climb diagonally up on to ridge and follow it NE to small hill overlooking Abernethy Glen. This hill was the site of an ancient fort.

Turn back and walk down N side of ridge a few yards to rocky track. Follow this WSW (254°) for about 250yd to its termination then descend steeply to the right beside forest until ground levels out a little before dropping off steeply again. At this point, enter forest and take indistinct path between trees down to grassy track. Go left along track, round a hair-pin bend, to a junction of paths; bear right (NE). After another hair-pin bend the track joins a gravel road and leaves the forest.

Turn left at crossroads then right on track then emerge on to main road (A912) opposite entrance to Glenfarg

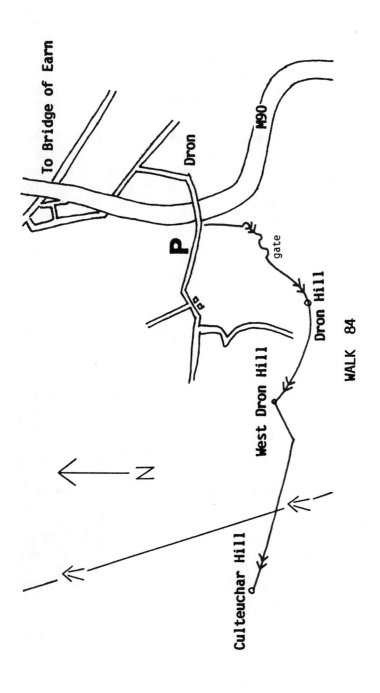

To Bridge of Earn

Dron

M90

gate

Dron Hill

West Dron Hill

WALK 84

Culteuchar Hill

N

House. Go NW along main road for about 300yd then turn left on to muddy farm track to T-junction at some farm buildings. Turn left, pass beneath old railway bridge then climb up on to track and return to starting point.

To shorten the walk, at Drumcairn take the farm track to the left down the valley and through the forest to the A912 then go N to rejoin the route at entrance to Glenfarg House. Save 2.1km/1.3ml.

84. *Earn Valley Escarpment*
Ordnance Survey map No: 58
Distance from city centre: 64km/39.6ml
Walking distance: 15.6km/9.4ml
Amount of climbing: 365m/1197ft

A walk along the escarpment overlooking the "Valley of the Kings". Views to Firth of Tay and Tay Rail Bridge. Terrain rough grassland, sheep and cattle grazing land.

Park on large flat area on edge of road between Dron and West Dron just after bridge over motorway. NO 135158. To get there, cross the Forth Road Bridge and take the M90 to jct. 9 then the A912 NW. At Bridge of Earn take the first road to left (unclassified) heading SE, pass beneath the motorway, then next right to Dron. Pass through the village and continue W to motorway bridge.

Walk back along road and turn right on to farm track just before motorway bridge. Follow this S beside a deep gully then SW over grazing land. The gully widens then divides into two. Just beyond this point, near a gas pipeline marker on the right, go through a wooden gate on right and climb SW over rough grazing land to top of Dron Hill (250m/820ft).

Descend WNW, cross a farm track coming up from the valley then climb West Dron Hill (291m/954ft). Head SW around top of gully and boggy area then WNW over hilly terrain, under overhead cables, and up on to Culteuchar Hill (313m/1026ft. TP). Retrace steps back to start.

It is not practicable to shorten this walk, other than by turning back before Culteuchar Hill.

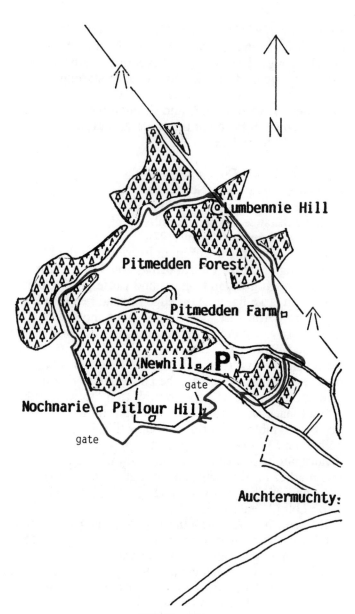

Lumbennie Hill

Pitmedden Forest

Pitmedden Farm

Newhill

P

gate

Nochnarie   Pitlour Hill

gate

Auchtermuchty:

N

WALK 85

85. Pitmedden Forest

Ordnance Survey map No: 58
Distance from city centre: 61.8km/32.4ml
Walking distance: 14.8km/9ml
Amount of climbing: 188m/616ft

A fairly easy walk over grasslands beside a deer farm then along forestry roads through Pitmedden Forest. There are a few fences to cross in the early part of the route.

Park in wide area before wooden barrier to forestry track near Newhill Farm. NO 218132. To get there, cross Forth Road Bridge and take M90 to jct. 8 then A91 following signs for St Andrews. At Auchtermuchty turn left on to B936 (signposted "Perth") then at fork (sign for venison on side of white building) go left into Mournipea and leave Auchtermuchty. Park in the third track into the forest on the right.

Pass through metal gate opposite parking area, turn left beside wall, climb over wooden gate and turn right beside fence to conifer plantation. Go left then right around the trees then continue WSW beside deer fence following it round to right and up on to Pitlour Hill (274m/898ft. TP on far side of deer fence).

Continue heading W (278°) alongside deer fence. At steep section deviate to left then bear right and descend to gate in corner of field. Enter field and head NNW (338°) beside hedge, past an abandoned homestead (Nocharie) then along edge of Pitmedden Forest.

Near corner of forest follow path between trees to forestry road (Shortcut 1). Go left along road for about 50yd then right (opposite open area on left) on to path heading NNW (335°) through forest. Join another forestry road and follow it round to right (NE) along edge of forest. Continue directly ahead, across crossroads (Shortcut 2) and two further junctions, to overhead cables. Here turn right, and follow cables through cutting to top of Lumbennie Hill (284m/931ft. TP).

Descend SE with overhead cables, across open ground

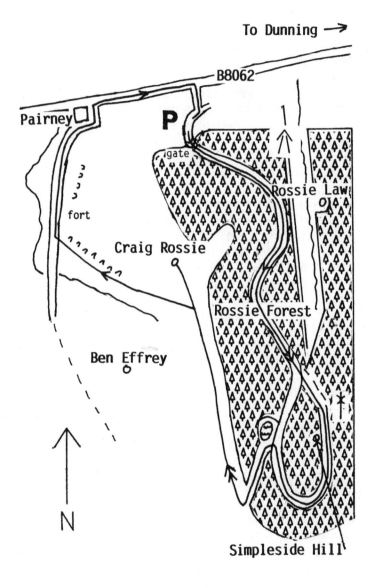

To Dunning →

B8062

Pairney

P

gate

Rossie Law

fort

Craig Rossie

Rossie Forest

Ben Effrey

Simpleside Hill

N

WALK 86

then back into forest and join track down to Pitmedden Farm. Walk down farm access road to junction then go uphill on road to sign for Craigard Cottage. Go left here, past cottage and through forest to another road. Follow road right to return to starting point.

To shorten the walk: (1) Go right, instead of left, along road to return past Newhill to starting point. Save 8.1km/5ml. (2) Turn right and follow forestry road to Pitmedden Farm. Save 1.3km/0.8ml.

86. Craig Rossie and Rossie Forest
Ordnance Survey map No: 58
Distance from city centre: 71.5km/44.2ml
Walking distance: 12km/7.5ml
Amount of climbing: 420m/1377ft

A stimulating walk through remote, rugged, forest and grass covered hills.

Park at beginning of access road to Rossie Forest. More spaces further along track for additional vehicles. NN986133. To get there, cross the Forth Road Bridge and take the M90 to jct. 6 then the A977 W, right on to B918 and left on A91 to Yetts o' Muckhart. Here join the A823, signposted "Crieff", then, in about 400yd, bear right on to B934 to Dunning then left on B8062 for 3.5km/2.2ml to track on left.

Walk along track S into Rossie Forest. Climb over gate and continue along gravel road through forest. The track runs beside a gully then swings right and later returns to gully. At this latter point, just beyond the end of overhead cables, leave the track and climb cutting through trees on left to prominent radio mast. Walk past the mast and join end of original road to top of Simpleside Hill (433m/1420ft).

Follow road as it winds its way down Simpleside Hill and round to the N. At a small loch turn back on yourself and descend SW through a fire break. On emerging from forest turn right and follow edge of woodland NNW up

211

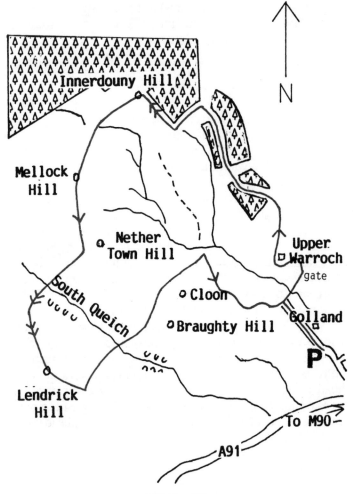

Innerdouny Hill

Mellock
Hill

Nether
Town Hill

Upper
Warroch

gate

South Queich

Cloon

Golland

Braughty Hill

P

Lendrick
Hill

To M90

A91

WALK 87

on to ridge. Continue NNW (335°) on to the crag-surrounded summit of Craig Rossie (410m/1344ft. TP).

Retrace steps down to shallow saddle below crags then descend W to join dirt farm track at bottom hill. Follow this N, past an ancient fort and some crags, then to the right of some farm buildings (Pairney) and over a wooden gate on to an asphalt road (B8062). Go right along road to starting point.

To shorten the walk, from Simpleside Hill, stay on gravel road, past loch, back down to starting point. Save 1.6km/1ml.

87. *Innerdouny and Lendrick Hills*
Ordnance Survey map No: 58
Distance from city centre: 48.8km/30.2ml
Walking distance: 22.5km/14ml
Amount of climbing: 672m/2204ft

An interesting circular walk over a number of small hills. There are many ascents and descents, some very steep, especially in and out of South Queich.

Park on edge of Golland Farm access road close to bridge over Golland Burn. Ensure sufficient space for the frequent lorries using the quarry to pass each other. NO058038. To get there, cross Forth Road Bridge and take M90 to jct. 6 then A977 W, right on to B918 and left on A91. Take next road right which is 1.7km/1.1ml after joining A91 and shortly after passing beneath overhead cables. It has a small entrance (easy to miss) and is not signposted. At bend go straight ahead on to Golland farm access road.

Walk along road. At fork just before Golland go right to farm, pass between two large barns and leave on track heading NW. At 90° bend in track turn right through gate and walk alongside stone wall, over beautiful stone bridge then beside burn to another farm track. Follow this uphill to farm buildings (Upper Warroch), walk around fence to far side and continue on track for further

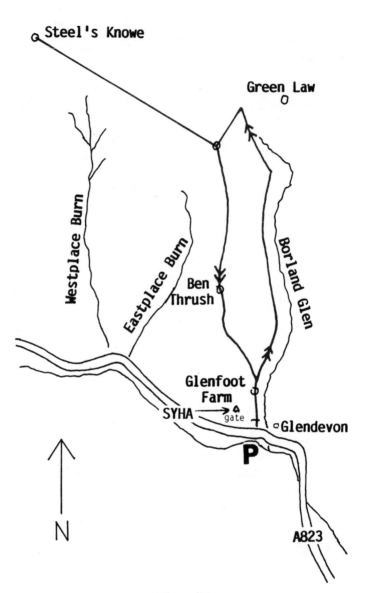

Steel's Knowe

Green Law

Westplace Burn

Eastplace Burn

Borland Glen

Ben
Thrush

Glenfoot
Farm

SYHA → gate

Glendevon

P

N

A823

WALK 88

50yd to junction of tracks. Here go right, following track uphill, through two small conifer plantations, as far as southerly projection of a more extensive forest ahead. Leave track and walk SW along edge of forest to corner then turn right and follow second side of forest on to summit of Innerdouny Hill (497m/1630ft. TP).

Cut down SW (234°), cross end of a gravel road and climb on to Mellock Hill (479m/1571ft). Descend southern ridge, pass over NW shoulder of Nether Town Hill then turn SW and descend steep sides of South Queich. Cross burn and fence in the bottom of the gully (approx 550yd from a main road) and climb the steep, grassy SW slope of South Queich to right of the crags. Once on ridge follow it SE to top of Lendrick Hill (456m/1495ft. TP).

Descend ESE (124°) to top of a gully then turn left (35°) and drop down in South Queich again. Climb far side, pass to left of Braughty Hill and Cloon, and descend to farm track. Follow edge of fields NE across valley to another farm track and follow this SE to Golland and on to starting point.

To shorten this walk, follow the gravel track below Innerdouny Hill down to Golland. Save 6.7km/4.1ml.

88.   *Ben Thrush and Steele's Knowe*
Ordnance Survey map No: 58
Distance from city centre: 57km/35.2ml
Walking distance: 14.2km/8.8ml
Amount of climbing: 369m/1210ft

A ridge walk to 1500ft over rough grassland.

Park close to entrance to Glendevon Youth Hotel (if possible). NN989046. (Additional parking at Castlehill Reservoir. NN996033.) To get there, cross the Forth Road Bridge and take the M90 to jct. 6 then the A977 W. Turn right on to B918 and left on A91 to Yetts o' Muckhart. Here join the A823, signposted "Crieff", as far as Glendevon.

Go through gate with signpost "Public Footpath to

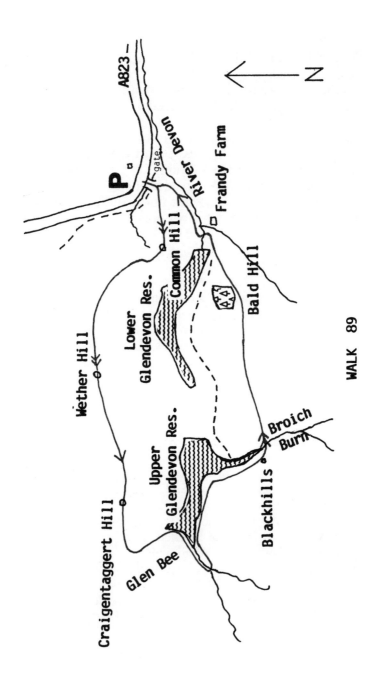

N

A823

P

gate

River Devon

Frandy Farm

Common Hill

Lower Glendevon Res.

Bald Hill

Wether Hill

Upper Glendevon Res.

Craigentaggert Hill

Glen Bee

Blackhills

Broich Burn

WALK 89

Auchterarder" and head N on track to Glenfoot Farm then footpath up Borland Glen to col. From here climb SSW (208°) to top of hill then follow ridge WNW (286°) down to saddle then up on to Steele's Knowe (485m/1590ft. TP).

Retrace steps as far as hill at SE end of ridge then swing round to the S, descend a little, then climb Ben Thrush (456m/1495ft). Descend S until gradient of descent diminishes then bear round to SE to descend to Glenfoot and return to starting point.

To shorten the walk, from hill above col, turn S towards Ben Thrush and omit ridge walk to Steele's Knowe. Save 6.4km/4ml.

89. Around Glendevon Reservoirs

Ordnance Survey map No: 58
Distance from city centre: 61.6km/38ml
Walking distance: 19.8km/12.3ml
Amount of climbing: 436m/1430ft

A walk over rough grassland on hills above the two Glendevon reservoirs returning on footpath along the southern shore of reservoirs.

Park in grass area on right of access road to Glendevon Reservoir, close to gate through stone wall. Space is limited. Unauthorised vehicles are not permitted beyond this point and there is nowhere to stop on the main road without causing an obstruction. NN949052. To get there, cross the Forth Road Bridge and take the M90 to jct. 6 then the A977 W. Turn right on to B918 and left on A91 to Yetts o' Muckhart. Here join the A823, signposted "Crieff", for 8.2km/5.2ml. The road to Glendevon Reservoir, signposted "Frandy Farm", is lined by a blue metal fence as far as gate through stone wall.

Go through the gate and immediately leave the track to climb NW up Common Hill (412m/1352ft). Descend NW by N (322°) to top of gully then climb broad, gently rising ridge ahead to its highest point, Wether Hill

(502m/1646ft). Continue W, across saddle, and on to Craigentaggert Hill (491m/1610ft).

Descend SW to join footpath at head of Glen Bee and Glen of Kinpauch. Follow path down Glen Bee then along western and southern shores of Upper Glendevon Reservoir to Blackhills. Now join track over Broich Burn and traverse northern flank of Bald Hill above Lower Glendevon Reservoir to dam wall and Frandy Farm. Continue on track over River Devon and back to starting point.

It is not practicable to shorten this walk.

Bridge over Warrock Burn on ascent of Innerdouny Hill : walk 87

West Lomond : walk 91

Glen Artney, Carn Labhruinn and ridge to Ben Vorlich : walk 97

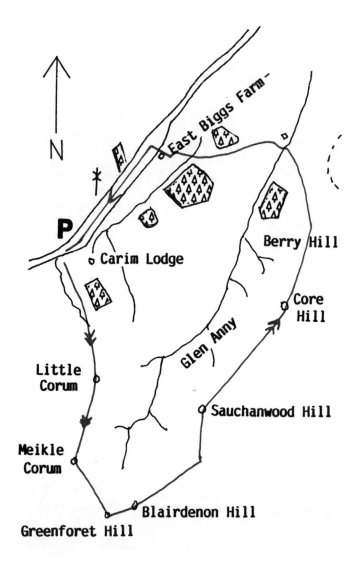

N

East Biggs Farm

P

Carim Lodge

Berry Hill

Core Hill

Glen Anny

Little Corum

Sauchanwood Hill

Meikle Corum

Blairdenon Hill

Greenforet Hill

WALK 90

90.   *Blairdenon Hill*

Ordnance Survey map No: 58

Distance from city centre: 75.5km/46.4ml

Walking distance: 20.5km/12.6ml

Amount of climbing: 588m/1928ft

A circular hill walk around Glen Anny in a remote part of the Ochil Hills.

Leave car on side of road between Carim Lodge and radio mast. NN857053. To get there, take the M9 then A9. At roundabout in Dunblane go right on to minor road following signs for Sheriffmuir. At T-junction next to Sheriffmuir Inn turn left. Carim Lodge is on the right just before a radio mast close to the road on left.

Head up to the right of the conifer plantation and continue S to top of Little Corum (520m/1705ft). Descend a little, climb Meikle Corum (596m/1954ft) then, heading SE, climb Greenforet Hill (616m/2020ft) and on to Blairdenon Hill (631m/2060ft). The route from Little Corum to this point follows the border between Tayside and Central Regions.

Descend the NE ridge, passing over Sauchanwood Hill, between Glen Anny and Fin Glen. Continue NE on to Core Hill (543m/1781ft) then swing gradually round to N and descend over Berry Hill and down ridge between two conifer plantations into Anny Glen. Cross burn and climb opposite bank to join a farm track on far side of ridge. Follow this W, through East Biggs Farm, to asphalt road. Go left along road, past radio mast, to return to parking place.

It is not practicable to shorten this walk.

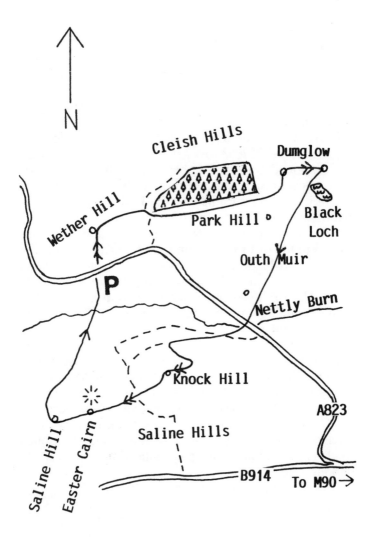

WALK 91

LOMOND HILLS AND CLEISH HILLS

91.   Cleish Hills and Saline Hills
Ordnance Survey map No: 58
Distance from city centre: 43.9km/27.2ml
Walking distance: 18km/11ml
Amount of climbing: 536m/1758ft

A short walk over a number of tops, with the early part a bit rough.

Park car on A823 (Dunfermline to Rumbling Bridge) near highest point. NT044952. To get there, go by Forth Bridge. At jct. 4 of M90 go W on B914 then A823 to Hillside.

Climb N to summit of Wether Hill (335m/1098ft). Then walk E along side of forest to Dumglow which has two tops (349m/1144ft and 379m/1243ft. TP).

Leave the Cleish Hills by descending SW past Black Loch and Park Hill, over Outh Muir to main road. Just S of the Nettly Burn go up track to West Lethans, turn left and up to summit of Knock Hill (364m/1193ft. TP. TV mast) – the first of the Saline Hills. Descend to the W and climb Easter Cairn (which has the remains of a fort) then across to Saline Hill (359m/1177ft). Return to car by going NNE (16°).

To shorten the walk, omit the Cleish Hills or the Saline Hills. Save 5.7km/3.5ml in either case.

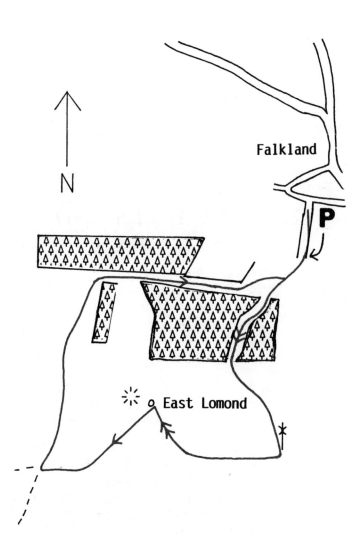

Falkland

P

East Lomond

WALK 92

92. *East Lomond*

Ordnance Survey map Nos: 58 and 59
Distance from city centre: 59.9km/37.1ml
Walking distance: 7.5km/4.6ml
Amount of climbing: 334m/1095ft

A short, steep hill walk over what was once the royal hunting grounds of Falkland Palace. The Palace and town of Falkland are also well worth exploring.

Park in East Loan, next to paper mill, Falkland. NO252070. To get there, cross the Forth Road Bridge and take the M90 to jct. 8, the A91 then A912, following signs to Falkland Palace. Pass the Palace entrance then turn left at the fountain with red lions into Cross Wynd. Continue S into East Loan and park.

Following the signs to Lomond Hills, walk S along a gravel road, round to the right past Lomondside Cottage then turn off left on footpath uphill through woodlands. On reaching open ground continue S on path until it turns WSW towards East Lomond. Turn off left here and head SE (144°) uphill over rough grassland and heather to radio mast (carpark, picnic site, viewfinder). Now take the signposted path W to the summit of East Lomond (424m/ 1390ft. TP. Viewfinder, site of ancient fort).

Head off WSW (240°) on the footpath which goes to Craigmead carpark. On reaching the old lime quarry, go N then NE around the base of East Lomond, on one of the many paths in the area, to a spur of trees rising up the hillside from the forest below. (NB: The mansion in the valley below is the House of Falkland, a school.) Descend down the W side of the line of trees, pass through at the bottom then use stile to enter forest. Go left for 3yd then right (E) on footpath through forest. Continue E on track (Fauld's Road) along edge of woodland to end of field on left. Turn left here, through bracken and over a gully, to join path used on way up.

To shorten the walk: (1) Follow main path direct to summit of East Lomond thus omitting the East Lomond picnic site. (2) Return on direct path from summit of East Lomond. Save 1.9km/1.2ml in either case.

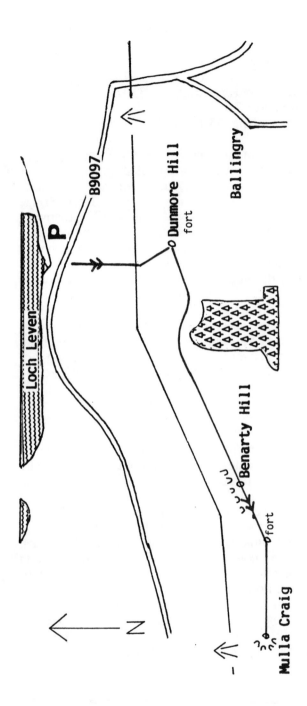

WALK 93

93. Benarty Hill

Ordnance Survey map No: 58
Distance from city centre: 41.8km/25.7ml
Walking distance: 12km/7.3ml
Amount of climbing: 331m/1085ft

A short walk to the top of a hill that stands out in fairly flat country. Provides superb views over Loch Leven, a nature reserve renowned for its bird life. The RSPB Centre at Vane Farm, close to the starting point, is well worth a visit.

Use carpark on southern shore of Loch Leven (also has toilets). NT170992. To get there, cross the Forth Road Bridge and take the M90 to jct. 5 then the B9097 E to Loch Leven.

Climb up shallow gully beside fence immediately opposite the carpark entrance until overhead cables are reached then head SE up on to Dunmore Hill (site of ancient fort). Head WSW (246°) along ridge then up grassy slope to forest. Go around the N end of woodland then follow stone wall W to summit of Benarty Hill (356m/1167ft. TP). Beware of sheer cliffs on north side of wall.

Continue W along top of crags to Mulla Craig (327m/1027ft). Retrace steps back to carpark.

It is not practicable to shorten this walk, other than by turning back before reaching Mulla Craig.

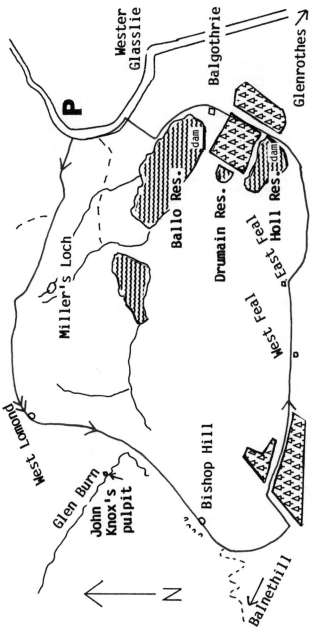

Wester Glasslie

P

Balgothrie

Glenrothes →

dam

Ballo Res.

dam

Drumain Res.

Holl Res.

Miller's Loch

West Feal

East Feal

WALK 94

West Lomond

Bishop Hill

Glen Burn

John Knox's pulpit

Balnethill

N

94.   West Lomond

Ordnance Survey map No: 58

Distance from city centre: 60.4km/37.4ml

Walking distance: 21.7km/13.5ml

Amount of climbing: 515m/1689ft

A circular walk around the escarpment and over the highest point of these prominent hills overlooking Loch Leven.

Use Craigmead carpark at highest point on road between Falkland and Leslie. NO227062. To get there cross the Forth Road Bridge and take the M90 to jct. 5 then follow the signs for Glenrothes. At Leslie turn left on to unclassified road signposted "Falkland". Craigmead is 5.6km/3.4ml along this road.

Leave the carpark through the gap in the fence near the toilets and follow track W to summit of West Lomond (522m/1712ft. TP). Descend the steep, southern side of West Lomond, cross rough grassland to Glen Burn then climb SW on to Bishop Hill. Note that there is a cave and prominent rock known as John Knox's pulpit lower down Glen Burn but a visit will entail a considerable loss of height.

Continue S along the escarpment, crossing path coming up from Balnethill, to the top of White Craigs overlooking the village of Kinnesswood. Now head NE along edge of woodlands to join path that descends E through the trees to West Feal then continue E on a track to Holl Reservoir. Cross the dam wall and follow path NNE through conifer plantation and over a small hill to Ballo Reservoir. Walk along the northern shore for 0.8km/ 0.5ml then take the path that heads NE up to a metal gate and asphalt road. Go left along the road to return to Craigmead.

To shorten the walk, retrace steps from West Lomond. Save 11.4km/7ml.

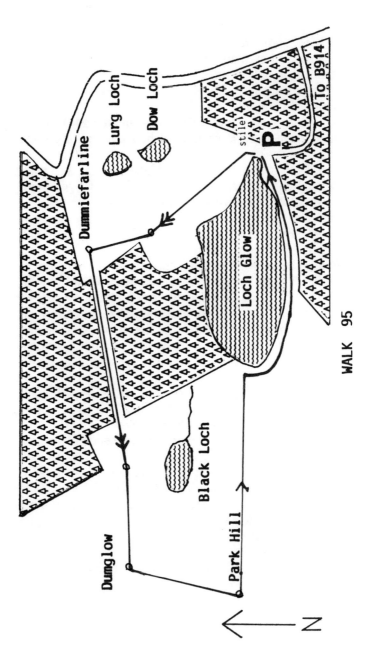

Lurg Loch

Dow Loch

Dummiefarline

To B914

stile

P

Loch Glow

WALK 95

Black Loch

Dumglow

Park Hill

N

95.   *Around Loch Glow*

Ordnance Survey map No: 58
Distance from city centre: 39km/24ml
Walking distance: 9.6km/6ml
Amount of climbing: 214m/702ft

A pleasant short walk through an area renowned for its bird life.

Park in small carpark at dam wall, Loch Glow. NT094957. To get there, cross the Forth Road Bridge and take the M90 to Jct. 4 then the B914 W. Take the next road right (unclassified) through forest to its highest point. Go through a wooden gate on the left (signpost "Loch Glow Reservoir") and drive along the gravel track to the loch.

Walk across the dam wall, climb the stile over a fence, then head NW (324°) over some low hills and on to the rocky top of Dummiefarline (336m/1102ft. Site of ancient fort). Now head W over rough grassland and through forest to Dumglow (379m/1243ft. TP. Remains of Pictish fort).

Continue W to second, slightly lower, summit of Dumglow then cross the shallow valley to the S and up on the Park Hill (330m/1082ft). Now head E to Loch Glow and follow the path around the southern shore back to the carpark.

It is not practicable to shorten this walk.

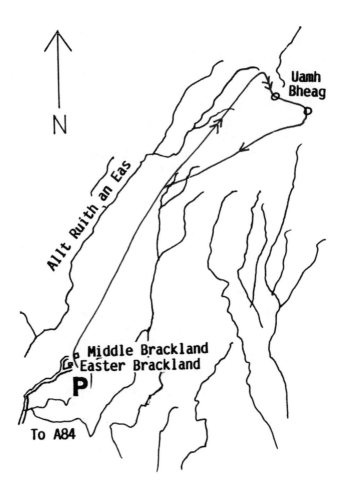

Uamh
Bheag

Allt Ruith an Eas

N

Middle Brackland
Easter Brackland

P

To A84

WALK 96

CENTRAL AND TAYSIDE REGIONS

96.   Uamh Bheag
Ordnance Survey map No: 57
Distance from city centre: 81km/50ml
Walking distance: 16.5km/10.2ml
Amount of climbing: 535m/1754ft

An unusual climb over rough moorland to a top giving good views and with some caves worth seeing.

Park car near Easter Brackland. NN663082. To get there, take the M9 to jct. 11. Turn left to Doune. Leave Doune on A84 towards Callander and at 9.4km/5.9ml from Doune at Dalvorich, turn right, then left and follow country road for 2.5km/1.7ml.

Walk up to Middle Brackland, then NNE (32°) steadily climbing to N end of top. Turn S and climb to top of Uamh Bheag (665m/2181ft). Cross over to second top, then descend towards the upward route. Return to start.

It is not practicable to shorten this walk.

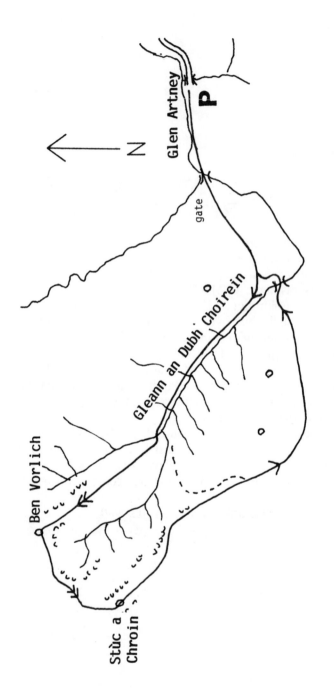

N

Glen Artney

P

gate

Gleann an Dubh Choirein

Ben Vorlich

Stùc a Chroin

WALK 97

97. Ben Vorlich

Ordnance Survey map No: 57

Distance from city centre: 95km/58ml

Walking distance: 36.3km/22.6ml

Amount of climbing: 1104m/3621ft

Ben Vorlich is a Munro, and although distant compared to most other routes described in this book, it is well worth the journey.

Leave vehicle in Glen Artney carpark. NN711161. To get there, cross the Forth Road Bridge and follow signs to Dunfermline then follow the A823 to Muthill (4.8km/3ml S of Crieff). Here go W on minor road past golf course. At T-junction turn right then, in 200yd left to continue W. Cross the B827 and drive for a further 2.3km/4.5ml along Glen Artney Road to carpark. Alternatively, although longer, it may be faster to take the M90 to Perth, the A85 to Comrie then the B827 S to the Glen Artney Road.

Continue on foot along the Glen Artney road past a vehicular turning space then through a gate across the road. Keep going SW along farm road to bridge over burn (Allt an Dubh Choirein). Do not cross bridge but head NW up glen (Gleann an Dubh Choirein) on right of burn, at first on a farm road then later on a path, until the valley divides into two. Climb the steep, narrow ridge between the two arms to the valley up to the rocky summit of Ben Vorlich (985m/3231ft. TP).

Head W off the summit for 500yd then turn SW and follow line of crags into col then up on to Stuc a'Chroin (972m/3188ft). From here there is a long, gentle ridge descent to the SE back into Glen Artney. At the bottom, follow farm road NE, across Allt an Dubh Choirein, and back to carpark.

To shorten the walk, return from Ben Vorlich summit by outward route (omit Stuc a'Chroin). Save 4.8km/3.1ml.

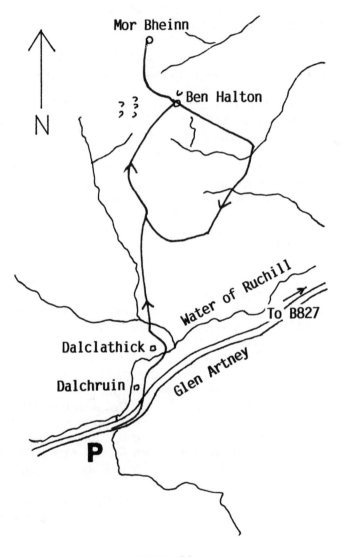

Mor Bheinn

Ben Halton

Water of Ruchill

To B827

Dalclathick

Glen Artney

Dalchruin

P

N

WALK 98

98. Ben Halton

Ordnance Survey map No: 57
Distance from city centre: 94km/58ml
Walking distance: 20.7km/12.7ml
Amount of climbing: 646m/2118ft

A pleasant climb in the foothills of the Grampian Mountains.

Leave vehicle in Glen Artney carpark. NN711161. To get there, cross the Forth Road Bridge and follow signs to Dunfermline then follow the A823 to Muthill (4.8km/3ml S of Crieff). Here go W on minor road past golf course. At T-junction turn right then, in 200yd left to continue W. Cross the B827 and drive for a further 7.3km/4.5ml along Glen Artney road to carpark. Alternatively, although longer, it may be faster to take the M90 to Perth, the A85 to Comrie, then the B827 S to the Glen Artney road.

Walk back along the road to Dalchruin. Fork left, descend to river (Water of Ruchill) and cross bridge to northern bank. Go downstream over bridge across a tributary then turn left and head N towards Ben Halton. At the base of the steep, grassy slopes you will find a hill road. Follow this N to its end then climb to right of crags on to summit of Ben Halton (621m/2036ft).

From Ben Halton head N through the many small hills and crags of Mor Bheinn to the TP (640m/2099ft) to the highest point. Return to Ben Halton then descend to the SE to rejoin the hill road. Follow this round to the S until the point at which the road was joined earlier is reached then take outward route back to the carpark.

It is not practicable to shorten this walk.

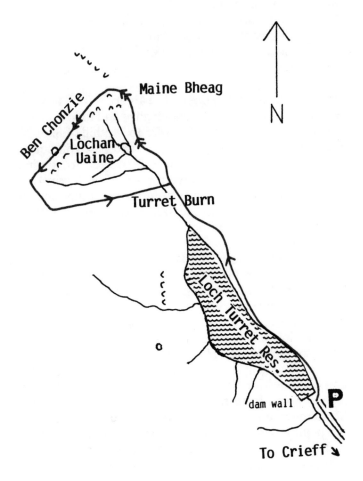

N

Maine Bheag

Ben Chonzie

Lochan Uaine

Turret Burn

Loch Turret Res.

dam wall

P

To Crieff

WALK   99

99. Ben Chonzie

Ordnance Survey map No: 52
Distance from city centre: 90km/55ml
Walking distance: 24.6km/15.4ml
Amount of climbing: 594m/1948ft

The line of mountains on each side of the initial level walk beside a reservoir provide a grand introduction to the climb to the high top, also known as Ben y Hone, which is a Munro.

Park car in large carpark at Loch Turret Reservoir. NN822265. To get there, take the M90 to Perth then the A85 to Crieff. Immediately on leaving Crieff and on crossing the Shaggie Burn, turn right up road beside the burn. Leave this road on left just after re-crossing the burn, and continue for 5km/3ml up to dam.

Walk along old road on E side of reservoir to its head, then along beside Turret Burn. Fork right above Lochan Uaine and climb up to Maine Bheag. Then steeply climb on to shoulder of mountain and turn along SW to top of Ben Chonzie (931m/3053ft), where three fences meet. Note the prevalence of mountain hares.

Return by SW for 750yd, then SE for another 750yd (marked "841" on OS map). From here strike due E to cross Turret Burn above reservoir. (If the burns are in spate it would be better to circle NE around Lochan Uaine, or to return from top by outward route.) Walk back along outward route.

It is not practicable to shorten this walk.

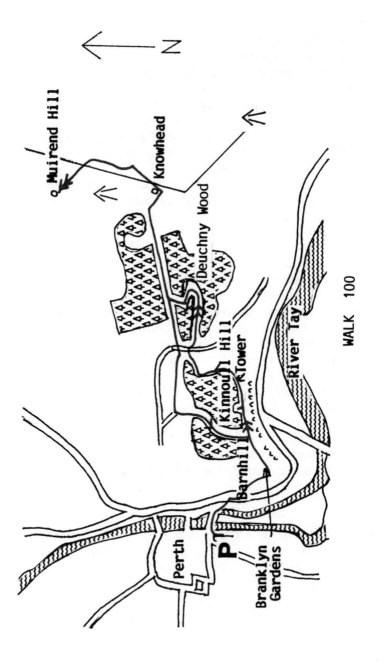

N

Muirend Hill

Knowhead

Deuchny Wood

Kinnoul Hill
Tower

Barnhill

River Tay

Perth

P

Branklyn
Gardens

WALK 100

100.   Kinnoull Hill

Ordnance Survey map No: 58
Distance from city centre: 68.3km/42.2ml
Walking distance: 25km/15.4ml
Amount of climbing: 362m/1187ft

A superb walk on hills overlooking the Tay Valley. The multitude of paths especially on Kinnoull Hill, make for endless route variations but may also make navigation difficult.

Park in large free carpark, with toilets, on banks of River Tay close to Perth city centre. NO120230. To get there, take the M90 then A912 from jct. 10 to Perth. At Inner Ring Road turn right then right again and right into carpark.

Walk upriver a little then cross River Tay using rail bridge. At main road on E bank go right then first left. Just before entrance to Branklyn Gardens (NTS), turn left then right at crossroads following sign for "Barnhill Cliff Views". This road soon becomes a track then narrow path. Follow it along top of cliffs, in and out of gullies, to highest point where there is a stone table (and superb view). A few paces away from cliff you will find summit of Kinnoull Hill (222m/728ft. TP. Two viewfinders).

Return to cliff and continue along edge on wide path signposted "Nature Trail". Soon you will reach Kinnoull Tower, perched precariously above the Tay. Follow path as it winds round glen overlooking Kinfauns Castle (seat of Earls of Moray). On reaching asphalt road, cross over, pass Jubilee carpark on left, climb over wooden barrier and follow forestry road SSE (150°). At hair-pin bend, leave road by continuing directly ahead on indistinct path through forest until eventually reaching a clearing. Go left for 100yd then left (W) along a forestry road to junction. Here go right (NNE) then right again (E) at a staggered crossroads. After 100yd at right-hand bend, go straight ahead on steeply descending path between trees to another forestry road (signposted "Coronation

Road"). Go right for a few paces then left (E) on path to edge of forest.

Head E over grazing land, passing a little to S of some trees, then down to some deserted farm buildings (Knowehead). Go round buildings then turn left (32°) and follow edge of fields beneath power lines to farm track. Walk along track to its end then go through metal gate and follow power lines until clear of trees on the left. Now cut up to left to prominent obelisk on summit of Muirend Hill (280m/918ft).

Retrace steps as far as staggered crossroads in Deuchny Wood. Here continue directly ahead (W) to reach asphalt road just N of Jubilee carpark. Cross over on to footpath through forest then farm access road and a few yards along main road. Go left on path up to viewfinder on Corsehill. Continue uphill between house and quarry (top of) to prominent crossroads. Go right to next junction of paths then ahead and to left to narrow path, traversing around the E of Kinnoull Hill, then down to Branklyn Gardens. (If lost, keep going to cliff edge then follow earlier route down.) Cross Tay back to carpark.

There are numerous short-cuts, e.g. turn round at Jubilee car park thereby omitting Deuchny Wood and Muirend (save 6.9km/4.2ml), or start and finish at quarry carpark (134234) thereby omitting steep climb up from city centre (save 13km/8ml).

AUTHORS' COMMENTS AND HINTS

GETTING TO THE START

The hill walks described in this book are based on the assumption that the walkers have the use of a car. Public transport is now quite inadequate. The cost of running a car for the relatively short distances is low when divided among the members of a party – much less than spending a whole day motoring. Some groups divide the cost of petrol used among those travelling in a car, while others take turns in providing the car. The former has the advantage that it provides, without any sense of obligation, for those who do not have a car or are not keen on driving.

An indication of suitable parking is given in each walk described. Be sure to avoid obstructing side roads or gates into fields. Leave space for heavy milk lorries, tractors, etc. to pass. But do not park on soft ground – it may be extremely difficult to get the car out when you return to it at the end of the day. If there is a house or farm nearby, advise the residents that you are leaving the car, in order that they will not be worried and perhaps inform the police.

Do not leave any loose objects on the seats or floor of the car – put them in the boot. Do not leave wallets or valuables even in the boot – take them with you.

Unfortunately, a few carparks have been invaded by car thieves. Check before closing up the car that the keys are in your possession and not in the car. A spare set handed to another member of the party is a good protection.

While the driver will not want to wear his boots for the journey, the others might do so if the boots are clean, and this will save the trouble of changing footwear at the start.

ACTION AND ATTITUDE

Hill walking is an acquired taste. Some get the habit when very young by being taken by their parents. Others learn to like it later. Many people never get the habit – even if they try. They cannot see the pleasure in putting on heavy boots, carrying a big rucksack, tramping over rough ground, accepting rain and even snow without running for shelter. But for the many who persevere and are bitten by the bug it becomes an essential part of life.

Regularity is important. For someone who is working, is only free at the week-ends, and has other social commit-ments, then once a month may be all that is possible. For retired persons and others, once a week is desirable. In any case it should at first be an obligation and it will gradually grow into a necessity – a delightful necessity, with pleasure when on the hills and satisfaction and good health thereafter.

While perseverance is part of the hill walker's attitude, never extend yourself beyond your capabilities. Do not go faster than is comfortable. Do not take risks. Do not be afraid to declare that you are tired or out of breath. Everyone feels like that at some time. However, it does pay a walker to acquire a steady pace with few stops.

Ideally one foot should be on firm ground before the other leaves the ground, and one should try to achieve this. But loose stones, slippery grass, ruts covered by heather can result in unsteadiness or even a fall. Good boots can, in such a case, save ankles from injury. Slight discomfort after such a fall will usually quickly disappear after walking for a minute or two.

CLOTHING

The choice of some garments may vary from person to person, but there are essential items if any enjoyment at all is to be had. The following notes illustrate this point:

Footwear – Boots with a solid, thick and gripping sole are essential. The uppers are usually of hard leather with tongue sewn up each side to prevent water penetration. Usually the uppers are sewn to the sole, but sometimes they are bonded. Fully waterproof boots are desirable, but seldom realized. Protection by waxing is advocated by some and condemned by others – it can help to keep water out but it can also rot stitching. After a day's soaking, stuff crumpled newspaper inside to absorb damp and maintain the shape.

Socks and stockings – Wear two pairs of thick wool socks or stockings – first a long pair up over the knee, second a short pair to fold over the top of the boots. Wear these when trying on boots for size.

Gaiters – For cold or wet days, gaiters are valuable. Nylon is preferred to canvas. The under-boot cords are unnecessary and should be removed. Ankle gaiters protect woollen socks and prevent stones getting into boots when walking in shorts or skirt.

Breeches or trousers – A pair of breeches or an old pair of trousers are equally suitable, provided they are strong and have good pockets (preferably with zip closures). They should not be tight-fitting.

Overtrousers – For very wet conditions, overtrousers with half-length zip side-openings are desirable.

Underwear – For winter, good thermal vest and pants are desirable, or two of each. In other seasons, it is a case of personal preference.

Shirt or blouse – A lightweight shirt or blouse of absorbent material with a breast pocket, open neck, and fold-over collar is desirable. The pocket for carrying an odd piece of equipment (compass, pedometer, etc.), the collar to catch the cord of a map case.

Pullover – A wool jumper should be taken along or worn. It provides warmth at higher altitudes, and, under a water-proof jacket, is a good absorber of perspiration.

Jacket – The purposes of the top garment are to retain the body heat, to stop cold winds penetrating, and to keep out the rain or snow. (Some people prefer two garments – one for warmth and a smock – over the head – for protection from rain). The jacket should be closed by means of zip fasteners and Velcro strips, should have good pockets with zip openings and flaps, and should have a hood tightened by a cord with cord grip.

Hat – A bare head or small wool hat is the choice for general wear, and a Balaclava covering ears and chin for very cold weather. In summer, a sunhat for those who suffer from sunstroke.

Gloves – Wool gloves with waterproof mitts provide warmth and protection. Since the mitts can be used when gripping all sorts of rough items (trees, rocks) they should be hard-wearing.

KIT

Travel light if you can but some kit is essential, especially in our climate and when you leave the roads and go into the hills.

Rucksack – The best way to carry what you must is in a light rucksack – not the large frame variety. Two side pockets are valuable – one for a vacuum flask and one for items hopefully not needed, such as first-aid, wallet, torch, etc. Do not rely on the rucksack being waterproof, so contain these items in a plastic bag. If the cord round the opening does not have a cord grip, fit one yourself

– in cold weather it is much easier to open and close. The shoulder straps should be adjusted so they won't slide off the shoulders of a nylon jacket – if necessary fix a cord round both of them, at the top, to draw them together.

Map – Always have a suitable map of the area you are covering – an Ordnance Survey 1:50,000 Landranger Series is recommended. For wet weather, carry it in a transparent map case slung round your neck and below the top layer of clothing. Study how to find a National Grid Reference.

Compass – Always carry a compass. It is frequently required for navigation and essential when unexpectedly enveloped in mist. Choose the type with bearings in degrees (e.g. Silva type) and make sure you know how to use it before setting out.

Whistle – Hopefully you will never need this, but in an emergency it could save your life by indicating your location. The International Distress Signal is six successive blasts repeated at one minute intervals.

First aid – Plasters, bandages, aspirins, cotton wool (to protect ears from biting winds), salted peanuts (to relieve cramp), and insect repellent (for midges) are all items which you should consider carrying.

Torch – Especially in winter, one can be delayed in the hills until after dark. This situation should be avoided, but if it is not, a torch is most valuable.

Food and drink – Some walkers like a good packed lunch for midday break, others eat little. It is advisable to have some sustenance. Carry it in a plastic box. Liquid refreshment could be tea, coffee, soft drink, etc. Boiling water in a vacuum flask, with tea bags carried separately, allows of a fresh cup of tea when required.

Spectacle case – If you wear spectacles, carry a case so that in mist, rain or snow you can remove your glasses in order to see your way.

Ground seat – At lunch break you will want to sit. You can, of course, sit on a waterproof garment, or you can get a small, slightly padded square specially made for the purpose which has a reflecting side to make use of the body heat.

Car keys – Always check before starting out on the walk that the car keys are carried in a secure pocket.

Wallet – Don't leave your wallet in the car. Put it in a waterproof cover and pack in rucksack pocket.

Pedometer – Few people will want to carry a pedometer, but if you do you should clip it in the breast pocket of shirt or blouse, and tie with cord to belt on trousers in case it slips out of pocket.

Walking stick – Some walkers find it helpful, especially in climbing up hills, to have a walking stick. If you do start taking one, try to have your name and address attached to it, since it is very easy to lay down and walk away without it.

Barbed-wire cover – Take a wad of newspaper, a piece of sacking, or a slit length of hose, so that it can be laid over barbed wire of a fence which must be crossed. A similar arrangement could be useful in crossing an electric fence. But be sure to avoid damaging the fence.

Ice axe – Despite name, use is not restricted to ice. Can be very useful when walking through snow. Determines depth and essential for arresting a slide down a snow-covered slope.

COMPANIONS

While a walk on the hills on one's own can be very enjoyable – solitude is, after all, one of the attractions of the open spaces – most walkers find company an added pleasure. Conversation when on a road or having a bite of food, or even snatches of talk when striding over the heather can be most satisfying.

Probably there should be three or four friends on an outing. Three provides a safeguard should a mishap occur. The victim with, say, a sprained ankle cannot move, the second can go for help, while the third stays with the injured party.

Groups of more than four require additional organization and preparation, a leader to set the pace and make route decisions, a large carpark and an established and previously reconnoitred route.

Above all go with persons with whom you can relax – companions, becoming friends. It does not matter whether they be male or female – mixed parties can be very successful.

There is the question of stamina. It is no use trying to maintain a group where one is willing and anxious to climb all the Munros in sight, while another is physically unable to do more than a flattish walk. There will always be variations (even within one person's own ability) but these should not be too great.

WEATHER

The only certain comment which can be made about weather in Scotland is that it is never possible, hour by hour, to say with certainty what it will be like. It can change from hot to cold, wet to dry, be exactly the opposite of the weather forecast, and it can change back and forth during one day. The message is, therefore, to prepare for the lot and hope for the best.

When it is mild in the city, it can be very cold a thousand feet up a hill. On the other hand, when the valleys are full of mist, the sun can shine with brilliance on the mountain tops.

If you go out walking on a regular basis, don't be put off by the weather. It can often turn out much better than it is early in the day. Apart from that, if properly protected, walking in any weather is a great enjoyment.

It is seldom that the weather is so bad that it is not possible to stop for a bite, sheltered from the rain or wind. In summer, if the sun is strong and warm, some people have to protect their head and skin; but at a higher altitude this is unlikely. In winter snows with a strong sun, however, protection is much more likely to be necessary, and dark goggles should be carried. Beware of mists – learn how to deal with them. Keep checking your compass bearings. Remember that mists greatly distort the appearance of distance and size; keep the party together. Heavy rain can quickly cause burns to be in spate and sometimes dangerous to cross. Unless you know of a bridge, go upstream until it is safe to go over.

Overcast skies can bring early darkness. It is always advisable to be back on a well-defined path or road before the sun sets, but if you are caught out use a torch, keep the party together, use your compass, and tread warily.

In a lightning storm, avoid standing on a peak, near a tree, or at the entrance to a cave. It is better to be flat on the ground than to stand up in an open flat area.

Keep a dry set of essential clothes in the car, so that if completely soaked a change is available in order to make the return car journey comfortable. It is not good for the health to travel in wet clothes, and this can apply also to perspiration. A rub down and a change of underwear can work wonders.

An accurate, local forecast issued by the Met Office and updated three or more times daily is available 24hrs daily by phoning the following numbers:

Edinburgh, S Fife and the Borders	0898 500 422
Southwest Scotland	0898 500 420
Glasgow, Clyde coast and Argyll	0898 500 421
Central, Tayside and E Fife	0898 500 423

SAFETY

The walks described in this book are not dangerous. There are no rock climbs, "bad steps", or raging torrents to cross. Nevertheless, mishaps can occur on the hills and sometimes with very serious effect. So it is advisable to take precautions.

1. Don't go when unwell.
2. Always have the proper clothing and kit.
3. Have a first-aid kit, and a whistle and torch.
4. Have food and drink. Warm drink unless the weather is very hot.

5.   Don't attempt more than you can manage.

6.   Don't go faster, to keep up with the others, if it is causing distress.

7.   Don't attempt to cross a fast-flowing burn unless you can have secure footholds.

8.   Don't walk over brittle rock, wet rock or icy rock.

9.   Only descend a steep slope if you are sure there are secure holds all the way down and a levelling out within a short distance should you slip.

10.   Keep in touch with your companions, especially where there is mist.

Probably the most dangerous part of your outing is when you are travelling in the car. So, take care on the road.

RIGHTS AND RESPONSIBILITIES

More correctly, it should be the other way round. Hill walkers have the responsibility of ensuring that they do nothing to harm the land and all that is on it. Always close gates, if you have opened them. Never walk on growing crops. Do not disturb farm animals or game (never take a dog with you). Respect walls and fences, even though the latter sometimes tear your clothes. Never leave litter, watching particularly when you stop for a meal. Do not light fires. Maintain the quiet of the countryside. Be extra careful when walking over sheep grazing land during the lambing season (in the Spring but varying with altitude), and avoid grouse moors during shooting (12 August to 10 December).

If you intend to park your car on, or walk through, private cultivated land, ask permission where this is feasible. Not only does the farmer or other local resident appreciate your doing so, but very often they give you good advice as to your route.

It is sometimes thought that in Scotland there is no law of trespass. This is not so. It is still possible to trespass, but you cannot be prosecuted for doing so. However, you can be sued for damage, and you can be asked to leave private ground. If so asked (and this happens very seldom), do so without question (unless you feel very strongly on the question of the freedom to roam on Scottish hills, and are prepared to face the consequences). We are fortunate that we have so many hills, almost all of which we are allowed to walk over freely. While this is what it should be, we must always remember our responsibilities to the countryside. "Rights of Way" are routes, through private property, over which the public have the right of passage. These are often marked as such. The Scottish Rights of Way Society Ltd does much to protect these, and deserves support from every hill walker. The best way to do this is to join and pay the very modest membership fee.

INDEX OF
PLACE NAMES

	Walk		Walk
Addinston Hill	16, 18	Cairnpapple Hill	4
Allermuir Hill	5	Canada Hill	45
Andrewhinney Hill	53	Capel Hill	51, 54
Annanhead Hill	60	Carleatheren	78
Arthur's Seat (Holyrood)	1	Carnethy Hill	6, 8
Arthur's Seat (Moffat Hills)	60	Castle Hill	69
Auchinstilloch	70	Castle Law	83
		Cleish Hills	91
Ballencleuch Law	66	Cloich Hills	55-57
Benarty Hill	93	Clover Law	58
Ben Chonzie	99	Cock Hill	73
Ben Cleuch	79	Cockleroy Hill	4
Ben Halton	98	Common Hill	89
Ben Shee	81	Core Hill	90
Ben Thrush	88	Corstorphine Hill	3
Ben Vorlich	97	Cort-ma Law	74
Ben y Hone	99	Craig Dod	65
Berry Hill	90	Craigengar	10
Binn Hill	83	Craigentaggert Hill	89
Birkscairn Hill	41, 47	Craig Rossie	86
Bishop Hill	94	Craik Cross Hill	50
Blackford Hill	2	Cramalt Craig	44
Black Hill (Ochils)	81	Cranshaws Hill	22
Black Hill (Pentlands)	12	Crawford Hills	69
Blackhope Scar	26, 27	Crow Hill	1
Blackhouse Heights	48	Culter Fell	68
Black Knowe	32	Culteuchar Hill	84
Black Knowe Head	49		
Black Law (Manor)	48	Dalmahoy Hill	14
Black Law (Moorfoots)	32	Deuchar Law	47
Black Meldon	56	Devil's Beef Tub	60
Black Mount	13	Dirrington Laws	21
Blairdenon Hill	90	Ditcher Law	18
Blythe Edge	20	Dollar Law	42
Bodesbeck Law	51, 54	Donald's Cleuch Head	59
Bore Stone	7, 9	Dron Hill	84
Bowbeat Hill	27, 34	Drumbuoy	73
Braid Hills	2	Drumelzier Law	43
Broad Law (Manor)	44	Dumbreck	77
Broad Law (Moorfoots)	29	Dumglow	91, 95
Broomy Side	58	Dummiefarline	95
Broughton Heights	58	Dumyat	80
Brown Knowe	38	Dundreich	27, 33
Byrehope Mount	10	Dungavel Hill	71
Byerside Hill	5	Dunmore Hill	93
		Dun Rig	41, 47
Cademuir Hill	46	Dunslair Heights	31
Caerketton Hill	5		
Cairn Law	44	Earl's Hill	76
Cairnoch Hill	76	Earl's Seat	77

	Walk		Walk
East Cairn Hill	9	Innerdownie	81, 82
Easter Cairn	91		
East Kip	6, 7		
East Lomond	92	Jeffries Corse	27
East Mount Lowther	64		
Eastside Heights	36	Kailzie Hill	41
Eildon Hills	40	Kaimes Hill	14
Emly Bank	27, 34	Kilsyth Hills	73
Ettrick Pen	54	King Seat	10
Ewelairs Hill	24	Kinnoul Hill	100
		Kirkhope Law	41
Fala Moor	30	Knock Hill	91
Fans Law	44		
Faw Mount	11		
Fennie Law	23	Laird's Hill	73
Fifescar Knowe	42	Lairs	74
Fintry Hills	72	Lammer Law	16, 17, 23
Firthhope Rig	59, 61, 62	Law, The	79
Firthybrig Head	59, 62	Lecket Hill	74
		Lees Hill	78
		Lendrick Hill	87
Gargunnock Hills	78	Little Auchinstilloch	70
Garrel Hill	73	Little Bin	75
Gathersnow Hill	68	Little Corum	90
Glengaber Hill	39	Little Says Law	15
Glenrath Heights	45	Lochcraig Head	59, 62
Glenstivon Dod	43	Loch Fell	52
Glenwhappen Rig	79	Lochlyock Hill	67
Greenforet Hill	90	Lomond Hills	94, 92
Green Law	58	Loup of Fintry	72
Green Lowther	64	Lowrans Law	23
Greenside Law	42	Lowther Hill	64
Grey Mare's Tail	61, 62	Lumbennie Hill	85
		Lylestone Hill	19
Hare Craig	70		
Hare Hill	6, 7, 12	Mauldslie Hill	26
Harehope Hill	57	Meikle Auchinstilloch	70
Harten Hill	71	Meikle Bin	75
Hart Fell	60, 63	Meikle Says Law	15
Hartfell Rig	63	Meldons	56
Hart Hill	76	Mellock Hill	87
Hartside Hill	28	Mickle Corum	90
Hawkwood Hill	69	Mid Rig	53
Heart Law	24	Minch Moor	37, 38
Herman Law	53	Molls Cleuch Dod	59
Hog's Law	19	Monynut Edge	24
Hope Hills	23	Mor Bheinn	98
Hundleshope Heights	45	Moss Law	68
Hunt Law	20	Mount Law	11
		Muirend Hill	100
Innerdouny Hill	87	Mulla Craig	93

	Walk		Walk
Nickies Knowe	59	Talla East Side	59
North Hart Law	19	Tarmangie Hill	81
Notman Law	42	Tewsgill Hill	69
Nutberry Hill	70	Tinto	67
		Tomtain	73
		Torfichen Hill	29
Park Hill	95	Torphichen Hill	4
Peat Law	19	Totherin Hill	67
Peniestone Knowe	53	Trowgrain Middle	53
Pentland Hills	5-6	Turnhouse Hill	6
Pitlour Hill	85	Twin Law	20
Porridge Cairn	44		
Priesthill Height	70		
Priesthill Law	22	Uamh Bheag	96
Pykestone Hill	43	Under Saddle Yoke	61, 63
Raggengill	69	Waddelscairn Moor	19
Ravengill Dod	65	Wanders Knowe	37
Riddel Law	19	Watchman's Brae	66
Roberton Law	71	Water Head	42
Rodger Law	66	Wedder Lairs	20
Rome Hill	69	Wedder Law	19
Rough Knowe	49	Wellgrain Dod	65
		Welshie Law	39
		West Dron Hill	84
Saddle Yoke	61, 63	Wester Dod	24
Saline Hills	91	West Hill	16, 17
Salisbury Crags	1	West Kip	6, 7
Sauchanwood Hill	90	West Lomond	94
Scad Hill	81	Wether Hill (Cleish Hills)	91
Scald Law	6, 7, 8	Wether Hill (Ochils)	89
Seenes Law	19	Wether Law	55
Simpleside Hill	86	Whinny Hill	1
South Queich	87	White Coomb	59, 61, 62
Spartleton	22	White Craig	10
Spout of Ballochleam	72, 78	Whitehope Knowe	60
St Abbs Head	25	Whitehope Law	35
Stake Hill	64	White Meldon	56
Stake Law	41, 47	White Shank	51, 54
Steele's Knowe	88	Whitewisp Hill	81, 82
Stob Law	45	Widow's Knowe	16, 17
Stronend	72	Windlestraw Law	36
Stuc a'Chroin	97	Windside Hill	35
Sundhope Height	49	Wood Brae	59
Swatte Fell	63	Wull Muir	29